# JOSEPH McCARTHY

# JOSEPH McCARTHY

## The Politics of Chaos

*Mark Landis*

Selinsgrove: Susquehanna University Press
London and Toronto: Associated University Presses

Associated University Presses
440 Forsgate Drive
Cranbury, NJ 08512

Associated University Presses
25 Sicilian Avenue
London WC1A 2QH, England

Associated University Presses
2133 Royal Windsor Drive
Unit 1
Mississauga, Ontario
Canada L5J 1K5

The paper used in this publication meets the
requirements of the American National Standard for
Permanence of Paper for Printed Library Materials Z39.48-1984.

**Library of Congress Cataloging-in-Publication Data**

Landis, Mark, 1946–
  Joseph McCarthy : the politics of chaos.

  Originated as a chapter of the author's doctoral
dissertation, Columbia University, 1973.
  Bibliography: p.
  Includes index.
  1. McCarthy, Joseph, 1908–1957.  2. Legislators—
United States—Biography.  3. United States. Congress.
Senate—Biography.  4. Anti-communist movements—
United States.  5. United States—Politics and
government—1945–1953.  I. Title.
E748.M143L26   1987      973.918′092′4[B]      85-63422
ISBN 0-941664-19-8 (alk. paper)

Printed in the United States of America

*To Jan*

# Contents

# Preface

This study originated as one chapter of my doctoral dissertation at Columbia University in 1973. Under the direction of Dr. James S. Young, that dissertation sought to test James David Barber's fourfold typology of political character and style by applying it to nine U.S. senators. One of those senators was Joseph McCarthy, and though the dissertation found his personality and behavior roughly consistent with that of the active-negative type Barber had delineated, some anomalies were noted.

Over the years, my interest in those anomalies grew, and I continued to wonder what might account for them. My interest in this problem led me first to the work of Abraham Maslow on need hierarchies, and then to the ideas of Jean Piaget and Lawrence Kohlberg on cognitive and moral development. R. W. Connell's work on the child's "construction" of the political world had a great impact on my thinking, as did Richard Merelman's analysis of the development of political ideology.

Increasingly, I saw an opportunity to build upon Barber's character/world view formulation by linking his concepts to the work of those mentioned above. James MacGregor Burns's 1976 presidential address to the American Political Science Association, suggesting that political leadership be studied from the perspective of needs and moral development, encouraged me to pursue this approach.

In one sense, therefore, there is nothing new being said about McCarthy in this volume, if by *new* is meant the uncovering of previously unkown facets of McCarthy's life or career. No hidden tape recordings have been unearthed, no secret memos found, no "smoking guns" discovered. Rather, I have been content to rely upon historians and biographers for the raw material I have tried to reinterpret in a useful way. Why did a struggle between political elites take on so hysterical and incoherent a tone? What was there about McCarthy himself that helped to create what came to be called McCarthyism? What accounts for McCarthy's rise and fall?

In the course of searching for answers to my question, I have accumulated a number of personal and intellectual debts I would like to repay in some small way by public acknowledgment. I want to give special thanks to Herbert Rosenbaum, William Levantrosser, Paul Harper, Bruce Adkinson, and Bernard Firestone (of Hofstra University's Political Science Department), and to Marilyn Shepherd (the department's secretary), for providing an environment that has never been anything less than stimulating and supportive.

On a personal note, I want to express my deep appreciation and gratitude for years of help and encouragment to my mother and my grandmother, and to my wife, Janis, who has helped me in more ways than I can even begin to count. I also want to thank my daughters, Karen and Jessica. While not exactly speeding the progress of this book, they always made me feel better about progress not made. Finally, I must pay tribute to the memory of my father, Jacob S. Landis. I think of the intense pleasure he derived from knowledge and learning, and I know why this book came to be.

# Acknowledgments

Thanks are due to the following publishers for permission to reproduce material from published works.

Beacon Press: From *McCarthy: The Man, the Senator, the "Ism,"* by Jack Anderson and Ronald May. Copyright © 1952 by Beacon Press. Reprinted by permission of Beacon Press.

Harcourt Brace Jovanovich, Inc.: From *Senator Joe McCarthy,* by Richard H. Rovere. Copyright © 1959. Reprinted by permission of Harcourt Brace Jovanovich, Inc.

The Free Press: From *A Conspiracy So Immense: The World of Joe McCarthy,* by David M. Oshinsky. Copyright © 1983. Reprinted by permission of The Free Press.

Stein and Day Publishers: From *The Life and Times of Joe McCarthy,* by Thomas C. Reeves. Copyright © 1982. Reprinted by permission of Stein and Day Publishers.

*Table 1.* American Political Science Review: From "Politics, Ideology, and Belief Systems," by Giovanni Sartori. Copyright © 1969. Reprinted by permission of the American Political Science Association.

*Table 2.* Melbourne University Press: From *The Child's Construction of Politics,* by R. W. Connell. Copyright © 1971. Reprinted by permission of Melbourne University Press.

*Table 3.* Yale University Press: From *The Lawmakers,* by James David Barber. Copyright © 1965. Reprinted by permission of Yale University Press.

# JOSEPH McCARTHY

# 1
## Interpretations of McCarthyism: Reconciling Pluralist and Elitist Views

### Analyzing McCarthyism

The rise of so controversial a figure as Joseph McCarthy in the period from 1950 to 1954 inevitably provoked intense debate within America's political, journalistic, and academic communities. The initial focus of dispute was, of course, McCarthy and his methods, and it centered upon the question of whether McCarthyism was a force for good or for evil. The outlines of that early debate can be seen in such representative works as Jack Anderson and Ronald May's *McCarthy: The Man, the Senator, the "Ism"* (1952) and William F. Buckley, Jr., and L. Brent Bozell's *McCarthy and His Enemies* (1954), which viewed the Wisconsin senator respectively as a dangerous demagogue and as a crusader for America's national security.[1] Probably the finest and most perceptive work to emerge from this tradition of analysis was Richard H. Rovere's *Senator Joe McCarthy* (1959).

It was not long, however, before more scholarly debate, aimed at a deeper understanding of the meaning of McCarthyism, began to develop. The focus in this debate was less upon the man, more upon the social phenomenon. The initial groundwork for such analysis was laid in a collection of essays edited by Daniel Bell and titled *The New American Right* (1955). Containing analyses by Richard Hofstadter, David Riesman and Nathan Glazer, Peter Viereck, Talcott Parsons, Seymour Martin Lipset, and Bell himself, the basic tenor of most of the pieces in this volume was that McCarthyism had to be understood as a manifestation of *mass politics*. From this perspective, McCarthyism represented a prime example of what would later come to be called "the irony of democracy"—the view that the greatest threat to democracy in America lies not in usurpation of power by an elite, but rather in the political mobilization of the masses.

Those who held that view came to be known as pluralists, and beginning in the mid- to late 1950s, McCarthyism was interpreted by them as symbolic of the worst excesses of mass politics. For this generation of students of American political history, the hysterical, irrational tone of McCarthy's anti-Communist crusade made it a worthy successor to such other mass (and hence quasi-fascistic) movements as Populism. McCarthy was viewed by the pluralists as exploiting popular resentments lying just below the surface of America's more traditional partisan politics. McCarthy's success up to 1954 seemed to such analysts virtually a textbook demonstration of what would happen should the masses ever become politically mobilized against the elites who maintained stability and liberty in the United States. It was the elites, they argued, who most strongly believed in the rules of the democratic game, and it was the masses who were least committed to such rules. Democracy's survival depended, therefore, upon keeping the masses quiescent.[2]

Such an analysis was, of course, not likely to remain long immune from challenge, and one of the most interesting aspects of the historical examination of McCarthyism stems precisely from its role in the debate over the validity of the pluralist conception of American politics. Thus, beginning in the early 1960s, closer examination of some of the survey data from the McCarthy era began to cast considerable doubt upon the accuracy of many of the commonly accepted ideas regarding mass support for McCarthy. Nelson Polsby in particular helped to shatter the myth that McCarthy had developed overwhelming public support for his cause in the early 1950s.[3] Earl Latham in *The Communist Controversy in Washington* (1966) urged that McCarthyism be viewed less in terms of mass sociology and more in terms of a weapon wielded by conservative Republicans in response to the frustration arising out of their unexpected defeat in 1948.

Finally, in 1967, Michael Rogin in *The Intellectuals and McCarthy* launched a major assault upon the entire pluralist analysis of mass politics, particularly as that analysis drew upon the evidence of McCarthyism. Not all mass movements were anomic and irrational, argued Rogin, nor did these characteristics invariably betoken mass, rather than elite, conflict. Indeed, concluded Rogin, McCarthyism itself could be much more effectively analyzed in terms of *elite conflict*—as nothing more than a continuation of normal partisan struggle in America.

For Rogin, McCarthyism did not emerge out of the agrarian radical roots of Populism, but rather as a partisan device harnessed by conservative Republican leaders to smash the New Deal coalition that had dominated American politics for the previous twenty years. The conclusion was clear—political activists and leaders were *not* the protectors of democratic values and principles against the masses. Given the right set of circumstances, elites were just as likely as the masses to lose their heads and trample upon civil liberties.

Ultimately, other approaches to McCarthyism were developed. Revisionist historians, viewing McCarthyism in the context of the Cold War, claimed to have found its roots in the actions of the Truman administration.[4] Some popular writers, looking back upon McCarthyism from the perspective of the Nixon-Agnew years, asserted that parallels between the two eras were of great significance for understanding the pattern of American politics.[5] A series of more specialized monographs examined McCarthy's relationships with his organized opposition and with such institutions as the Catholic Church and organized labor.[6] Most recently, the role of President Eisenhower in the senator's downfall has become a focus of inquiry. The thesis has been set forth, for example, that—far from being a passive spectator refusing "to get into the gutter with that guy"— Eisenhower played a shrewd and influential role in McCarthy's political demise.[7] Thus, it is clear that the fascination with Joseph McCarthy, both as man and as phenomenon, endures.

### Elite Conflict, Mass Style

Even if one were to accept the preponderance of evidence that shows McCarthyism to have been primarily the product of an elite partisan conflict, an important problem remains to be resolved. One cannot help but feel that although the empirical truth may indeed lie with the critics of the pluralist view, there is nonetheless at least a symbolic truth that belongs to the pluralists. Clearly the pluralists were responding to *something* that caused them to feel that McCarthyism was rooted in mass political behavior. More specifically, it appears that it must have been the chaotic, irrational, and hysterical nature of that era that caused them to regard McCarthyism as a mass movement.

Here, then, is the gist of the problem: If McCarthyism was indeed an elite rather than a mass phenomenon, how then to explain its tone or style? The conflict of party elites in the United States, whatever else may be said about it, has not generally been characterized by attacks on the opposition party as traitors. Indeed, a major conclusion of almost every study of the development of democracy in early America has concerned the central role played by acceptance of the idea of a "legitimate opposition."[8] With the Civil War period and its aftermath as the one notable exception, attacks on the opposition party as traitors have not been commonplace in American politics, at least since the early 1800s. Yet quite clearly this *was* at the heart of McCarthyism, and thus it becomes important to try to understand why this particular elite conflict should have taken so unusual a turn.

If the Republican party in the late 1940s had concluded that anti-Communism was a useful partisan weapon, it would not have been terribly

surprising. If arguments had been made, for example, that the Democrats—caught up in the warm glow of the wartime alliance against the
Axis—had been insufficiently alert to the dangers of Communism at
home, it could have been viewed as not very different from the usual
partisan fare. But McCarthyism obviously represented something considerably different, something more than the mere use of anti-Communism as
a traditional political issue. It meant, instead, something like the assertion:

> The Democratic label is now the property of men and women who have
> . . . bent to the whispered pleas from the lips of traitors . . . men and
> women who wear the political label stitched with the idiocy of a
> Truman, rotted by the deceit of an Acheson, corrupted by the red slime
> of a [Harry Dexter] White.[9]

The claim, therefore, was not just that the opposition party was stupid,
incompetent, wrongheaded, or venal, but that its tenure in office actually
constituted, in McCarthy's most famous phrase, "twenty years of treason."

And yet if one were to conclude from statements so grim as the above
that McCarthy was simply a "true believer," caught up in a genuine
ideological crusade—perhaps somewhat more extreme and paranoid than
most—one would be quite wrong. For just as unusual as the powerful
content of McCarthy's charges was the rather offhand approach he took in
developing those charges. Far from being a serious, determined hunt for
Communists in government, McCarthyism resembled nothing so much as
a circus or carnival. And if, therefore, it seems strange that charges of
treason would be leveled against the opposition party in what appears to
have been a conflict between elites, it is perhaps even stranger to find such
charges developed in so casual and irrational a manner. McCarthy's hit-
and-run approach to finding "Communists in government," his random
choice of targets, the insubstantiality of so much of his evidence, his
willingness to drop investigations that yielded insufficient press
coverage—all seem distinctly removed from the world of elite political
conflict as it is normally conceived. In the words of one author, "when all
due reverence has been paid to the damage done by McCarthyism, it still
retains that aura of incredible nonsense."[10]

Thus, although one probably ought not to be surprised that the Republican party seized upon anti-Communism as a partisan issue in the
1950s (indeed, other Republicans had tried to make use of it before
McCarthy), one should be surprised, first that the issue was defined in a
way so dangerous to the fabric of American politics, and second that it was
exploited in so bizarre and erratic a manner. While it is certainly true that
elite conflict in America has often been rough-and-tumble, a sense of limits

and at least a vague framework of rationality have normally prevailed. McCarthyism, on the other hand, seems to have represented a kind of political brawling with no limits—a politics of no holds barred and anything goes—and at the same time, an astonishingly casual approach to political battle. For a man who claimed to believe that the U.S. government was riddled with subversives and that the dominant political party of the day had been seduced by traitors, McCarthy certainly did not appear to invest much care or thought in developing a coherent strategy for defeating the enemy in this titanic struggle. Indeed, what was most striking about McCarthy's approach was its very haphazardness and spontaneity, the sense it produced of random flailing about.

It is here then—in the political style of Joseph McCarthy—that one finds the elements of what pluralists identified as the style of mass politics. Yet it is found in the form of a U.S. senator, at the level of elite conflict. Thus, the argument to be developed here is that it is the personality and style of Joseph McCarthy that serves as the explanatory link reconciling this seeming contradiction of mass style and elite conflict.[11] Only by bringing McCarthy himself back into the study of McCarthyism can one hope to make sense of a puzzling era in American history. Both pluralists and their critics, it can be argued, have come to focus so much of their attention upon the context of McCarthyism—whether at the mass or elite level—that the very man who gave his name to the phenomenon has tended to recede somewhat into the background. But McCarthyism cannot really be understood without restoring McCarthy himself to a central role in the study of that era.

While no one can doubt that the political environment of America in the 1950s helped to foster and sustain McCarthyism, the environmental explanations that have been put forward over the years are really best suited to explaining how and why anti-Communism became so important a political issue. Now needed is the corrective of focusing more strongly upon Senator McCarthy in order to begin to understand why that issue came to be used in the odd manner that it was. While the political environment of 1950s America is useful in explaining the anti-Communist content of McCarthyism, it does not explain its chaotic, irrational style. It was the injection of Joseph McCarthy's political style into the elite partisan struggles of the period from 1950 to 1954 that gave the anti-Communist issue its peculiar force, but also ultimately proved its undoing (see table 1). Anti-Communism, it seems almost certain, would have been an important force in 1950s American politics even without Joseph McCarthy, but it would not have been McCarthyism as the term came to be known. Indeed, anti-Communism without McCarthy might well have been more rational and sophisticated and perhaps, in the long run, a far more dangerous threat to American civil liberties. Thus, it is not surprising that, initially at least,

TABLE 1
FACTORS SHAPING MCCARTHYISM

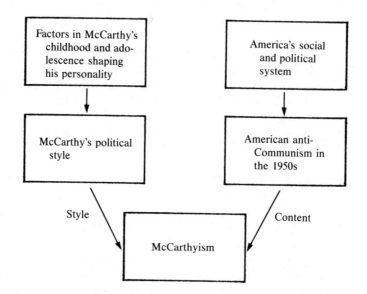

"Richard Nixon and other members of the House Un-American Activities Committee considered [McCarthy] a disaster."[12] But of course McCarthy left little choice in the matter. He imparted a special flavor to his era, and it is only by coming to understand McCarthy himself that one can hope to understand the meshing of mass style and elite conflict that he brought about.

It would, of course, be foolish to suggest that McCarthy's role in McCarthyism has gone completely unnoticed. Michael Rogin, for example, has argued that "it is important to stress McCarthy's uniqueness," particularly as regards "his thoroughgoing contempt for the rules of political controversy" and his "willingness not to play by the rules."[13] Another political scientist has asserted that

> what seems decisive was that a particular senator, with a set of personal needs and goals, and a distinctive set of ideas about how to fulfill those needs and achieve those goals, assumed the direction of the committee.[14]

Yet, while there has certainly been recognition of McCarthy's catalytic role, there has been relatively little attempt to develop systematic ideas about how and why McCarthy came to play his part. What is necessary now, therefore, is an attempt to understand the significance of McCarthy's political style. What was the nature of that style? What were its psychological dynamics? What were its origins?

## Methodology

If one accepts the idea of Joseph McCarthy as the crucial link between the elite conflict and the mass style that characterized McCarthyism, it becomes important to understand the nature of his political style. This in turn requires some insight into its manner of operation and how it came to be put together in the first place. Inevitably, therefore, one focuses upon McCarthy's personality, and this kind of study has traditionally been regarded as subject to dangerous pitfalls.

It has been widely argued, for example, that attempts to predict behavior on the basis of personality have proven relatively unsuccessful.[15] What makes this study more likely to be successful in linking personality and behavior is its emphasis on one aspect of personality—style. As Fred Greenstein has argued, "Even when there is little room for personal variability in the instrumental aspects of actions, there is likely to be variability in their expressive aspects."[16] Personal style, he notes, is one such expressive aspect. Thus, while it is normally true that a subject's behavior is likelier to be determined by the specific situation in which he finds himself than by his personality, there does remain greater room for personal variability in such aspects as the style of behavior adopted by the subject. Because my concern here is primarily with *how* McCarthy dealt with the issue of "Communists in government," there is good reason to believe that a systematic analysis of McCarthy's personality might yield some useful insights into the nature of the McCarthy era.

In approaching the problem of McCarthy's political personality, an initial theoretical organizing perspective is essential. Twenty years ago, political psychologists would have regarded someone like Joseph McCarthy as prime material for retrospective psychoanalysis. A journey through the realms of psychopathology would have been viewed as the likeliest way to untangle the complex strands of so confusing a personality. But one of the major problems with psycho-history and psycho-biography has been their tendency to develop idiosyncratic, particularistic explanations for the behavior of the subject under study.[17]

It might not be difficult, for example, simply to label McCarthy in terms of some pathology and then to treat him as a unique case. Ultimately, however, it should prove more valuable to attempt to understand him in terms of some broader theoretical framework that can enable him to be placed into psychological context. Therefore, in order to avoid another study of only limited applicability, it ought to prove advantageous to approach the case of Joseph McCarthy with something on the order of a "preliminary theory" that can serve as a methodological anchor, restraining one from generating further ad hoc explanations with no value beyond the one subject under examination.[18]

Employing a comprehensive and plausible prior theory should, therefore, permit one to take advantage of a reciprocating process that will strengthen both the case study of Senator McCarthy and the conceptual framework brought to the study. The case study will have to submit to the rigor demanded by the prior theory, while the theory itself will have to come to grips with the "inconveniences" of the empirical data.

In the late 1960s and early 1970s, moving away from psychoanalytic models for the study of political personality, James David Barber's work on American presidents demonstrated the value of social psychological approaches—in particular something akin to the psychology of adaptation—for understanding the shaping of the personalities of political leaders.[19] Moreover, Barber's approach was precisely to focus upon the element of "style"—the linking element that seems so central to a proper appreciation of Joseph McCarthy's role in the shaping of McCarthyism. Style was viewed by Barber as a useful conceptual tool for understanding the connection between deeper, more fundamental aspects of personality on the one hand, and actual behavior on the other.

> "Style" in this context means a collection of habitual action patterns in meeting role demands. Viewed from the outside, a man's style is the observed quality and character of his performance. Viewed from inside, it is his bundle of strategies for adapting, for protecting and enhancing his self-esteem.[20]

Barber's main hypothesis was that the style a political leader adopts can be predicted, at least roughly, from a knowledge of how his character developed in childhood and how his world view developed in adolescence. *Character* was defined by Barber as the way a subject "orients himself toward life—not for the moment, but enduringly."[21] While not used in this framework as a psychoanalytic term in the strict sense, character was seen, in one analysis of Barber's work, as providing "at least a link to, and a reflection of, unconscious needs, ego defenses, and psychodynamics."[22] Character development was therefore to be viewed as that phase of personal development when levels of self-esteem were determined, thereby shaping the extent to which future behavior would be based upon the need to compensate for early ego deprivations.

*World view,* Barber suggested, could be seen as consisting of a subject's "primary, politically relevant beliefs, particularly his conceptions of social causality, human nature, and the central moral conflicts of the time."[23] How a person looked at the world around him would obviously play a significant role in how he reacted to it. Here then, the focus was upon beliefs, attitudes, and values rather than upon needs and motives.

The character and world view developed in the process of maturation would, according to Barber, constitute the raw materials out of which a politician's style would come to be built. Style would crystallize in the period of "first independent success," and variations in style would in all likelihood

> be linked to the experiences in early adulthood of the man's first inde-
> pendent success, that period of style adoption in which he found
> marked infusions of confidence from relative success, a relatively new
> and special relationship to group life, and a relatively sudden emergence
> from obscurity to wider attention.[24]

The way in which one emerged onto the public stage was profoundly important, therefore, and significantly shaped the manner in which one's life strategies developed. By pulling together the strands of character development, building of a world view, and style adoption in the period of first independent success, one could perhaps begin to approach a fuller understanding of a subject's functioning in the political arena.

This approach, then, will constitute the skeleton of the prior theory for the study of the personality and style of Senator Joseph McCarthy. My focus will be upon his political style, and I will be particularly concerned with understanding the nature of that style's operation in the political process, the psychological dynamics underlying it, and the factors that gave rise to it. Although building upon the work of James Barber, I expect to deepen the value of that framework by linking it to the work of such major scholars as Abraham Maslow, Jean Piaget, and Lawrence Kohlberg, somewhat in the manner recently proposed by another student of political leadership, James MacGregor Burns.[25]

In the course of this study, major reliance will be placed upon the work of the main biographers of Joseph McCarthy for the data that will be examined. As regards the main outlines of McCarthy's public career, I am dealing with a figure who received close coverge during his lifetime and who was very much in the public spotlight for five crucial years. McCarthy's political style has therefore been quite meticulously documented in earlier works.

Although the details of McCarthy's youth remain considerably sketchier than those of his public years, recent scholarship has shed some new light on old assumptions.[26] At the very least, those who wish to understand McCarthy are no longer forced to rely upon accounts developed by journalists over thirty years ago. McCarthy's private papers remain closed to scholars, but there is reason to believe that, when opened, they will reveal relatively little about his youth that is not already known.

Thus, it is probably reasonable to conclude that virtually all that will ever be known regarding the details of Joseph McCarthy's life is known now. What remains, therefore, is the task of interpretation—shaping the bits and pieces of data available into a coherent framework with the explanatory power to make sense of the contradictions and anomalies of McCarthy's political behavior.

## Notes

1. Jack Anderson and Ronald May, *McCarthy: The Man, the Senator, the "Ism"* (Boston: Beacon Press, 1952); William F. Buckley, Jr., and L. Brent Bozell, *McCarthy and His Enemies* (Chicago: Henry Regnery, 1954). Other works in this tradition include James Rorty and Moshe Decter, *McCarthy and the Communists* (Boston: Beacon Press, 1954); Roy Cohn, *McCarthy* (New York: New American Library, 1968); and the chapter on McCarthy in Reinhard Luthin, *American Demagogues* (Boston: Beacon Press, 1954).

2. A full-blown statement of this view can be found neatly expressed in Bernard R. Berelson, Paul F. Lazarsfeld, and William N. McPhee, *Voting: A Study in Opinion Formation in a Presidential Campaign* (Chicago: University of Chicago Press, 1954), chap. 14, "Democratic Practice and Democratic Theory."

3. Nelson W. Polsby, "Toward an Explanation of McCarthyism," *Political Studies* 8 (October 1960): 250–71.

4. Athan Theoharis, *Seeds of Repression: Harry S. Truman and the Origins of Mc-Carthyism* (Chicago: Quadrangle, 1971); Richard M. Freeland, *The Truman Doctrine and the Origins of McCarthyism* (New York: Alfred Knopf, 1971). A countering view can be found in Alan D. Harper, *The Politics of Loyalty: The White House and the Communist Issue, 1946–1952* (Westport, Conn.: Greenwood Press, 1969).

5. Fred J. Cook, *The Nightmare Decade: The Life and Times of Senator Joe McCarthy* (New York: Random House, 1971); Robert C. Goldston, *The American Nightmare* (Indianapolis: Bobbs-Merrill, 1973); Roberta S. Feuerlicht, *Joe McCarthy and McCarthyism: The Hate That Haunts America* (New York: McGraw-Hill, 1972).

6. Donald F. Crosby, *God, Church, and Flag: Senator Joseph R. McCarthy and the Catholic Church, 1950–1957* (Chapel Hill: University of North Carolina Press, 1978); David M. Oshinsky, *Senator Joseph McCarthy and the American Labor Movement* (Columbia: University of Missouri Press, 1976); Richard M. Fried, *Men Against McCarthy* (New York: Columbia University Press, 1976).

7. See Fred I. Greenstein, *The Hidden-Hand Presidency: Eisenhower as Leader* (New York: Basic Books, 1982), chap. 5; and William Bragg Ewald, Jr., *Who Killed Joe McCarthy?* (New York: Simon and Schuster, 1984).

8. Richard Hofstadter, *The Idea of a Party System: The Rise of Legitimate Opposition in the United States, 1740–1840* (Berkeley and Los Angeles: University of California Press, 1970). On the theoretical point, see Seymour Martin Lipset, Martin Trow, and James S. Coleman, *Union Democracy* (Glencoe, Ill.: Free Press, 1956).

9. Richard Rovere, *Senator Joe McCarthy* (New York: Harcourt, Brace, 1959), p. 11.

10. Goldston, *American Nightmare*, p. 189.

11. What is here termed *mass style* may indeed be far from the exclusive property of the masses if such analyses as that of Michael Paul Rogin, *The Intellectuals and McCarthy: The Radical Specter* (Cambridge: MIT Press, 1967), are correct. The use of the term *mass style* to describe irrational, incoherent patterns of thought and behavior does, therefore, take on a pejorative tone. A more neutral term, such as *unconstrained style*, might be preferable.

12. Rovere, *Senator Joe McCarthy,* p. 135.

13. Rogin, *Intellectuals and McCarthy,* pp. 252, 251.

14. Leroy N. Rieselbach, *Congressional Politics* (New York: McGraw-Hill, 1973), p. 36.

15. Fred I. Greenstein, *Personality and Politics* (New York: W. W. Norton, 1975), p. 34.

16. Ibid.

17. Betty Glad, "The Role of Psychoanalytical Biography in Political Science," *American Political Science Association Annual Meeting* (Washington, D.C., 1968).

18. Alexander George, "Some Uses of Dynamic Psychology in Political Biography: Case Materials on Woodrow Wilson," in *A Source Book for the Study of Personality and Politics,* ed. Fred I. Greenstein and Michael Lerner (Chicago: Markham, 1971), p. 81.

19. James David Barber, *The Presidential Character: Predicting Performance in the White House* (Englewood Cliffs, N.J.: Prentice-Hall, 1972).

20. James David Barber, "Classifying and Predicting Presidential Styles: Two 'Weak' Presidents," *Journal of Social Issues* 24 (July 1968): 52.

21. Barber, *Presidential Character,* p. 8.

22. Alexander George, "Assessing Presidential Character," *World Politics* 26 (January 1974): 241.

23. Barber, *Presidential Character,* pp. 7–8.

24. James David Barber, "The President and His Friends," *American Political Science Association Annual Meeting* (New York, 1969), p. 13.

25. James MacGregor Burns, *Leadership* (New York: Harper and Row, 1978), chap. 3.

26. Thomas C. Reeves, *The Life and Times of Joe McCarthy* (New York: Stein and Day, 1982); David M. Oshinsky, *A Conspiracy So Immense: The World of Joe McCarthy* (New York: Free Press, 1983).

# 2
## Joseph McCarthy: A Biographical Sketch

### Early Life

Joseph Raymond McCarthy was born in Grand Chute Township, Wisconsin, in 1908. His grandfather, Stephen, born in Ireland in 1821, had lived for a time in upstate New York, and then moved to Grand Chute in 1859. There he married the daughter of Bavarian immigrants and fathered ten children. One of these children, Timothy McCarthy, married Bridget Tierney in 1901, and settled down to farm the land given him by his parents. Tim and Bridget's fifth child was Joe McCarthy.

Timothy McCarthy's 142-acre farm lay in the heart of a section known as the Irish Settlement, an enclave in a region otherwise dominated by German, Dutch, and Scandinavian settlers. Tim and Bridget (known as "Bid") were intensely pious Roman Catholics, frugal and hardworking. One neighbor recalled: "Tim worked all the time. And he expected his boys to do the same. He was a serious fellow."[1] One biography suggests that the McCarthy's life "was a continuous round of work relieved only by an occasional visit with neighbors, and by Sunday worship at St. Mary's Church in Appleton, seven miles away."[2]

But if there is general agreement that hard work was at the center of the McCarthy family's life, there is considerable question about how to characterize the nature of Joe McCarthy's formative years. On this subject, two competing accounts exist.

The older tradition—established almost thirty-five years ago by Jack Anderson and Ronald May in their generally hostile study of McCarthy's career—contends that young Joe endured a deeply unhappy childhood on his parents' Wisconsin farm.[3] Three more recent studies, on the other hand, conclude that McCarthy's childhood was a relatively normal one.[4] "In terms of what is known about his class, religion, upbringing, and education," concludes one, "there seems to be little that sets Joseph Raymond McCarthy apart from his boyhood peers in and around 'the Irish Settlement.'"[5]

Anderson and May, on the basis of their research and interviews in the early 1950s, described a Tim McCarthy who "taught his seven children that the only important things in life could be found on their rolling acres, in the crops and cattle."[6] In this version, Joe McCarthy did not get on well with his father, an exceptionally demanding man whose main goal in life seemed to be insuring that his sons turned out as much like him as possible. Even Roy Cohn, McCarthy's aide and friend, had little to say about Tim McCarthy beyond that he was a "stern disciplinarian."[7]

As a contrast to Timothy, and perhaps by way of providing an explanation for Joe's intense ambition, Anderson and May presented Bid McCarthy as a woman who babied her son, consoling him when he sought refuge from the harsh teasing and the fighting of his older brothers. They depicted Tim scolding his wife for mothering the boy excessively. One historian described how

> Mother Bridget McCarthy threw a special protective wing around the shy, sulky boy, and when the rough testing came, he sought out her big warm apron. "Don't you mind," she would console. "You be somebody. You get ahead."[8]

Roy Cohn offered a somewhat different perspective on this relationship, suggesting that while Joe was indeed his mother's "special pride," in reality, she "did not pamper Joe but prodded him to 'get ahead,' to 'be somebody.'"[9] While somewhat different, this second account seemed to offer mainly a shift in emphasis.

Anderson and May suggested a third element important to an understanding of Joe's personal development. They described an exceptionally unattractive child. With shaggy eyebrows, downturned lips, big chest, and short arms, McCarthy is said to have resembled a bear cub, and to have received an inordinate amount of taunting on this score from his older brothers.[10] A demanding father, an overprotective mother, and physical unattractiveness that made him the butt of ill-treatment—all combined to account in rather simple (not to say simplistic) psychological terms for Joe McCarthy's political personality.

Presented in such a manner, McCarthy's early life, though perhaps not painfully harsh in purely material terms (the family seems to have been of about average economic status), nonetheless was made to seem unusually bleak and unhappy. In support of that view, Richard Rovere—a journalist who followed McCarthy's career closely—could not help but point out that, in *McCarthyism: The Fight for America* (the closest McCarthy ever came to writing an autobiography), the senator devoted virtually no space at all to his childhood. How many other politicians, Rovere wondered, would have passed up the opportunity to talk of a family that began in a log

cabin and of the splendid character development available to those growing up on a farm?[11]

Nor did Anderson and May's story end with their depiction of family
tensions. In their version, McCarthy's school years saw him turning increasingly inward, shunning others, and burying himself in books. His
sister remembered him reading library books late into the night, even
though he was required to arise before six to do his chores. His introver-
sion was so great—in this account—that

> The neighbors remember Joe as a shy lad, seen-but-not-heard. One
> woman recalls that whenever her family visited the McCarthys, Joe
> would be nowhere in sight.[12]

Sometimes, young Joe would even hide in order to avoid having to meet
visitors. And the same tendency was evident in school:

> Although he did well in his early school years, and even skipped a grade,
> young Joe never felt comfortable under the teacher's gaze, nor enjoyed
> frolicking on the swing and teeter-totter at recess with the other chil-
> dren. And he was so self-conscious that he could hardly find his voice
> when it came his turn to recite.[13]

There were times when Joe would ask his teacher for permission to step
outside for a moment and then would run home to his mother. According
to Anderson and May:

> His former playmates say he entered into their games . . . only with
> reluctance, and his feelings were easily hurt. They say that, as long as
> they knew him, he never really learned how to play.[14]

At fourteen, then, McCarthy was graduated from the Underhill Country
School, according to Anderson and May, "a stubby, morose child, strong
for his age, who shunned the company of others. Bullied by his brothers,
cowed by old Timothy, the young boy found refuge only in his mother."[15]
Having completed the eighth grade, young Joe McCarthy, formerly so
enthralled by books, now wanted to leave school. His teachers had seen
the boy who once had been able virtually to memorize his textbooks come
to pay less and less attention in class as he took to daydreaming. Young
Joe did quit school, and soon he was working full-time in his father's fields.
But "after a few months under the heavy hand of Timothy McCarthy,
young Joe began to display outwardly an antipathy toward his father,"[16]
Anderson and May report. He evolved a plan that would allow him to
escape. Joe accumulated sixty-five dollars by working part-time for his
uncle, and then rented an acre of land from his father (paying standard

rates). On this land, McCarthy set up a chicken farm. Within two years, he had built his sixty-five-dollar investment into two thousand laying hens and ten thousand broilers, a chicken house, and an old truck.

This period in McCarthy's life, as he sought to match himself against the model provided by his father, and proved himself worthy, might have become his "first independent success"—the period Barber describes as the time when a politician's future style crystallizes. It was certainly a time of considerable personal satisfaction for the young man. Anderson and May describe how Bid McCarthy worried about her son when he began driving his products to the Chicago markets.

> So to show his mother how he stood in the world of men, Joe put her in his truck, and took her to Chicago with him: a sixteen-year-old boy, driving a man's truck, doing a man's job, taking his mother across the Wisconsin state line for the first time in her life. It was the high point of Joe's young life; but the triumph was to be short-lived.[17]

Working twelve to fourteen hours a day, seven days a week, plowing all his profits back into his business, McCarthy finally overextended himself. He fell sick and had no money to pay a professional to watch over his chickens. Too proud to turn to his father or his brothers, McCarthy hired two local boys to care for the poultry. The two boys were not especially interested in chickens, and while Joe McCarthy lay sick, most of his empire was wiped out. Five years of work was destroyed in a few weeks' time. Faced now with the choice of starting all over or of finding a new line of endeavor, McCarthy chose the latter course. The slow retracing of familiar steps was considerably less appealing than a bold leap into a new, uncharted realm.

Joe McCarthy's trips away from home during the time he had raised chickens had brought him into contact with a wider world. Even in the immediate area, the local poultry king had made the acquaintance of such worldly people as bartenders, gamblers, and various young men about town. Now he looked forward to a new life, away from the farm, with a chance to find a real place for himself in the scheme of things.

And so, in 1929, Joe McCarthy piled a few belongings onto his truck, and drove thirty miles away to Manawa—a town of only a few thousand citizens, but big by comparison to the backwoods. On the basis of the portrait painted by Anderson and May, one can not regard this as anything but McCarthy's escape from an oppressive home environment.

This outline of McCarthy's life up to age twenty has always had the virtue of appearing to make sense of what was to follow. Indeed, so tempting were the easy conclusions one could draw from Anderson and May's version, that as early as 1959, Richard Rovere (while accepting the broad outlines of their findings) nonetheless felt compelled to warn that "in the little that is known of McCarthy's childhood and youth, there is nothing that is singular enough in nature to account for this singular man."[18]

In the 1980s, that warning blossomed into a full-scale attack upon Anderson and May's conclusions. Michael O'Brien, Thomas Reeves, and David Oshinsky each returned in 1976/77 to the scenes of McCarthy's childhood, and talked to neighbors, friends, and family members, seeking to assess the accuracy of what Anderson and May had reported in 1952. Each concluded that there was considerable reason to doubt whether the two had presented a sufficiently balanced picture of McCarthy's early life.

O'Brien concluded that speculation on the causes of McCarthy's behavior was "based on insufficient and sometimes contradictory data."[19] Reeves asserted quite bluntly that "what we know about Joe McCarthy's childhood does not really explain his subsequent conduct."[20] Oshinsky, while acknowledging that "the recollections of friends and neighbors are always suspect" (the ones he spoke to, no less so than the ones found by Anderson and May), concluded that the report of an unhappy childhood for McCarthy were "based on guesswork and wishful thinking, nothing more."[21]

On the basis of his research, Reeves concluded that "the McCarthys were a close, happy family—hard-working, very religious, proud of their ancestry, distinctive in no readily observable way from other families in the strip of farms called 'the Irish Settlement.'"[22] Indeed, "Joe was an almost totally extroverted boy, loud, fun-loving, constantly in the thick of things, and extremely popular."[23]

Oshinsky reported that family friends were struck by "the genuine affection between Joe and his parents," that "Joe may well have been Tim's favorite," and that neighbors remembered Joe as "a vigorous, extroverted, ruggedly handsome boy."[24] He did exceptionally well in school, his main problem being a tendency to "cause a stir by blurting out the right answer" when older students were too slow.[25] Although Oshinsky thought it possible that some friction might have developed between father and son in the year that Joe quit school and worked on the family farm, he found no evidence of any deep-seated problem.

The conflict between Anderson and May's account, on the one hand, and that of O'Brien, Reeves, and Oshinsky, on the other, presents obvious difficulties for anyone seeking to understand McCarthy's personality. Which version is one to believe? Each of these biographers interviewed friends, neighbors, and family, but radically different stories emerged. Perhaps the quarter-century gap between the two sets of interviews made a difference. Perhaps different sets of friends and neighbors had different impressions of the McCarthy family. Perhaps one interviewer or another allowed bias to intrude.

In the end, it is probably Oshinsky who offers the most balanced assessment. He acknowledges that those who adhere to the belief that McCarthy could not have had a "normal" childhood "may well be right," although "the best *available* evidence, admittedly superficial, points in another direction."[26]

In sum, one appears to have a choice between a somewhat more dubious picture of an unhappy childhood (but one that could help to account for McCarthy's later behavior), and a marginally more plausible picture of a normal childhood (but one that makes it considerably more difficult to account for that later behavior). As Robert Griffith pointed out in a review of Reeves's book:

> McCarthy's behavior—the reckless gambling, the prevarications, the alcoholism, the vulnerability to injury and illness—seems to cry out for explanation. What were the springs of McCarthy's behavior? There is no answer in this incomplete biography.[27]

Surprisingly, however, the biographers' divergent views regarding McCarthy's childhood cause less difficulty for the analysis of McCarthy's political personality than one might imagine. This is so because the question of McCarthy's early life is relevant primarily to only one aspect of the study of political personality—genesis.

Fred Greenstein has suggested that the study of personality can be conducted from three different and analytically separable perspectives: *phenomenology* (the description of regular patterns of behavior—the "presenting symptoms," so to speak); *dynamics* (theoretical explanations for how the intrapsychic processes operate to shape behavior); and finally, *genesis* (the origins of the intrapsychic processes that produce the behavior).[28] Thus, one can seek an understanding of Joe McCarthy's motives and of his world view without necessarily having to explain how they came into being. Such an understanding, even without a theory of genesis, would still be no small accomplishment.

Moreover, one need not, in any event, totally surrender the possibility for genetic explanation. Certainly if one accepts Anderson and May's account of a significantly abnormal childhood, such explanation seems well within the realm of possibility. And even from the perspective of the O'Brien, Reeves, and Oshinsky versions, it remains possible to assert that factors other than interfamilial tensions could have contributed to the shaping of McCarthy's political style.

Oshinsky is certainly correct in asserting of Joe McCarthy that "the inner dynamics of his youth—his dreams and fears, his deepest feelings about Tim and Bid, and theirs about him and themselves—will never be known."[29] Still, this is a far cry from asserting that McCarthy's later political conduct is completely unexplainable, for as Oshinsky also points out:

> We have little knowledge of other influences that may have been at work. The Irish, for example, were a minority in Grand Chute, surrounded by people who often viewed them as less than equal. The McCarthys were very provincial; when Joe went to Appleton, friends remember, the children would tease him about his bib overalls, bringing tears to his eyes.[30]

Although one might not care to build too grand a theoretical edifice upon the few hints contained in that paragraph, it certainly suggests that family problems need not be the only explanatory variable considered in seeking the roots of McCarthy's style.

### First Independent Success (and Beyond)

James David Barber defines the period of first independent success as the "clearly discernible period, usually in late adolescence or early adulthood, in which a style is adopted."[31] It is a time of emergence to wider attention, a time of developing confidence, a time of finding a new relationship to group life. Typically, a confluence of motives, resources, and opportunities produces a personal style—"a collection of habitual action patterns in meeting role demands."[32] This style will be resorted to again and again when meeting the challenge of political office.

Until he left for Manawa in 1929, Joe McCarthy could have been best characterized in terms of intense drive and ambition and a willingness to work hard to achieve his goals. Raised in the farming tradition of his father, McCarthy had found a ready outlet for his intense energies in the demanding work of cultivating a farm, and later, of raising chickens. No doubt he was prepared to approach his new life in Manawa in the same way. "It is clear, however, that a sudden and dramatic change occurred in McCarthy's life just about the time he was achieving his majority—when he moved from rural Grand Chute to the little Waupaca County village of Manawa in the spring of 1929."[33]

McCarthy found a job in Manawa as the manager of the local branch of the Cashway grocery chain. And whether one believes with Anderson and May that McCarthy had till then been shy and introverted, or with Reeves and Oshinsky that he was already outgoing and extroverted, there is no doubt that in Manawa McCarthy flowered. The opportunity to deal with

debating tournament, McCarthy stopped to meet some small-town judges, explaining only that it "might do me some good later."[57] McCarthy, who had never before displayed any interest in politics, was perhaps beginning to give it some thought.

McCarthy finished his law studies in 1935, was admitted to the Wisconsin bar (no state bar examination was required), and immediately opened his practice in Waupaca, the county seat of Waupaca County, and therefore a place that offered political opportunities for a newcomer. McCarthy shared his first office with a dentist, and it soon became evident that most of the money was being made by the dentist. In the six months of 1935 that he practiced, McCarthy handled four cases and earned less than eight hundred dollars.

Before long, McCarthy could regularly be found in the back room of Ben Johnson's bar on Highway 10, running up his poker winnings. A fellow lawyer who participated in those sessions recalled that "he'd take all the fun out of the game, because he took it so seriously."[58] A friend recalled, "You get to the point where you don't care what McCarthy's got in the hole—all you know is that it's too costly to stay in the game."[59] On the other hand, there were times when

> he would cheat at cards, and roar with laughter when caught. It wasn't for the money; he merely wanted to see what he could get away with.[60]

With a mixture of ferocity, cheating, and bluff, McCarthy was able to win the occasional large pot, and to make ends meet.

McCarthy's reputation as a lawyer was not very good. "He was what you'd call an ambulance chaser," a local attorney recalled. "He'd do things no other lawyer in town would think of doing, like shading you out of a case, talking behind your back to your own client."[61] But McCarthy's focus was shifting from law to politics anyway, and to that end he became an inveterate joiner and speechmaker. He became a member of the Junior Chamber of Commerce, the Lions Club, a local softball team, and other small groups. He willingly accepted all the small chores that might eventually bring him a reputation as a community leader. If a committee needed to be chaired, tickets sold, or a speech given, McCarthy was always available.

Early in 1936, Mike Eberlein, a successful Republican lawyer from Shawano, Wisconsin, dropped in on McCarthy and offered him a job at fifty dollars a week. The next morning at eight o'clock, McCarthy was in Eberlein's office, announcing to the startled receptionist, "I'm your new boy. You watch; in a few years I'm going to be on the top of the heap around Shawano."[62] With his salary of two hundred dollars a month, a bachelor like McCarthy should have been able to live quite comfortably in

Shawano, and yet he was always in debt. Finally, Eberlein arranged to give McCarthy only one hundred dollars a month and twelve hundred dollars in one lump sum at the end of the year, but even this did not solve McCarthy's financial problem. "Some of the money," Anderson and May reported, "was dissipated in a constant attempt to buy political prestige. Joe picked up tabs at luncheons, and he kept in the public eye by promoting speaking engagements whenever he could."[63] Robert Griffith concludes that "the association with Eberlein gave McCarthy security and a place in the community, but the older lawyer was strict and domineering and McCarthy was soon searching for new outlets for his great energy."[64]

In August 1936, McCarthy was elected president of the Young Democrats of the Seventh Congressional District. Soon thereafter, he announced his candidacy for district attorney of Shawano County. McCarthy campaigned energetically in the open primary, but with only 577 votes he ran third behind the Progressive incumbent (3,014 votes) and the Republican (692 votes). It was immediately clear that McCarthy's chances for victory in the November general election were nil, but he decided to use the two months left of the campaign to make a reputation for himself. He campaigned intensively, making numerous speeches attacking his opponents. In November, the Progressive candidate received 6,175 votes to McCarthy's 3,422 and the Republican's 2,842. McCarthy's political stock rose sharply as a result of this showing. Moreover, "the furious activity and the slashing attacks had appeared to pay off. Joe would not soon forget this lesson in campaigning."[65]

For the next two years, McCarthy remained a partner in Eberlein's firm, but continued to seek a political opening. He dropped out of most Democratic party activity by 1938, although he did not formally change his affiliation. Instead, he seized upon the opportunity to contest a nonpartisan office early in 1939. An election was to be held for a judgeship in the Tenth Judicial Circuit of Wisconsin, and McCarthy decided to challenge the incumbent, Judge Edgar Werner.[66]

McCarthy quickly launched an energetic campaign, driving around in a car with a loudspeaker on top, shaking every hand in sight, visiting every farm, and mailing out thousands of postcards to voters.

Every responsible politician in the three-county area labeled McCarthy's candidacy a farce. He had barely turned thirty; he was probably the least experienced lawyer in the district, and he lacked the dignity a judge should have.[67]

But McCarthy hit upon a tactic that proved extremely promising. He began to refer to his opponent as a seventy-three-year-old man, much in need of rest from his public labors. Although Judge Werner appears actually to have been sixty-six years old, he made the mistake of falling on the defensive, arguing the merits of age and experience.

Rovere concludes that it was in this campaign that

> McCarthy had become liberated from the morality that prevailed in his environment, in his time, in his profession. It was not the fact that he lied that revealed this . . . it was McCarthy's surpassing boldness, in some ways even the grandeur of his falsehoods, that set him . . . apart from ordinary misrepresentation.[68]

For Rovere, McCarthy's singularity lay not in the fact that he would lie to win an election, but that he would lie even when the truth was easily accessible to everyone.[69] When McCarthy triumphed over Werner by 15,000 votes to 11,000 votes, the lesson must have seemed plain to him. And though protests were filed against McCarthy's tactics, they came to nothing, and in January 1940, McCarthy took office.

As a judge, McCarthy was—not surprisingly—exceptionally energetic. His court reporter often could not keep up with him, and within a few months, the new judge had cleared up a considerable court backlog. In one stretch of forty-four days, Judge McCarthy kept his court in session past midnight a dozen times. In addition, when he discovered that it was common practice for judges on occasion to trade circuits, McCarthy quickly developed such trading to a fine art, to allow himself to travel all over the state at public expense.

Whenever he came to a new area, McCarthy would look up the lawyers, judges, and newspapermen; on future visits he would always drop by to pass the time of day.

> But it was to newspapermen that he was most cordial. Some reporters kept a careful watch on the court rosters to see when their friend Joe McCarthy would arrive to pick up the tabs at the swankiest places in town. He became known all over the state as the most generous, dynamic, nose-to-the-grindstone judge on the bench.[70]

Yet almost from the beginning, McCarthy's judicial career was embroiled in controversy. He was criticized for granting "quickie" divorces, sometimes without even a court clerk present, and once on the courthouse steps.[71]

A more serious matter was McCarthy's conduct in a case involving the state agriculture department versus the Quaker Dairy, a firm engaged in price-cutting, in violation of Wisconsin's price floors for milk. McCarthy first granted an injunction against Quaker's practices, but then quashed it. He explained that although the dairy had indeed broken the law, to enforce it would work a hardship against the company—and besides, the law would soon expire anyway. Therefore, it would be a "waste of the court's time" to try such a case.

When the agriculture department appealed this decision to the Wisconsin supreme court, Judge McCarthy was ordered to send up all records of the case. The stenographic record arrived with one page torn out. When the high court demanded an explanation, McCarthy explained that he had deemed the excised portion "immaterial." The Wisconsin supreme court overturned McCarthy's ruling and issued a scathing denunciation of his conduct in the matter. Ironically, however, McCarthy actually benefited from the affair, winning recognition as a consumer hero and a foe of price-fixing state bureaucrats.[72]

A few months later, the United States entered World War II, and McCarthy decided to seek a commission in the Marines. All of McCarthy's biographers seem to agree that this spurt of patriotism was generated, at least in part, by a sense of the political advantages to be reaped, and perhaps by a need to keep up with Carl Zeidler, the glamorous young mayor of Milwaukee, who had immediately enlisted in the Navy.[73]

Although he had immediately applied for an officer's rank, McCarthy informed the press that he would enter the Marines as a buck private. For years afterward, McCarthy would contend that he had entered the Marines as a private, and that he had "earned" a lieutenant's commission. In fact, he was directly commissioned a first lieutenant in July 1942.

Moreover, rather than resigning his judgeship, McCarthy agreed only to waive his judicial salary while in the service. He prevailed upon the other circuit court judges to handle his cases while he was gone, although this arrangement greatly disturbed the chief judge, who saw a heavy burden being thrown upon the other judges. In any event, after trying his last case dressed in a Marine uniform (with newspaper photographers specially invited for the occasion), McCarthy was off to Quantico for training.

McCarthy remained in the Marine Corps from July 1942 until December 1944, when he resigned his commission. Most of that time was spent as an intelligence officer in the Pacific, interviewing pilots upon their return from bombing missions. On occasion, McCarthy would insist upon joining a bombing run as a rear gunner, although most of the pilots obviously preferred someone with more experience for that job. McCarthy quickly earned something of a reputation as a wild and overeager shot. This did not stop a constant flow of stories back to Wisconsin, telling of "Tail-Gunner Joe" who, for example, set a military record in 1943 by firing 4,700 rounds of ammunition in one day. Unfortunately for the U.S. war effort, most of it seems to have been aimed at coconut trees.

In 1943, on the basis of a letter he forged, McCarthy won a citation from Admiral Nimitz for devotion to duty despite his "severe leg injury." According to a shipmate, McCarthy sustained the injury going down a ladder with a bucket on his foot, as part of a shipboard initiation rite.[74] One of McCarthy's fellow officers later told Anderson and May:

> That guy could promote anything up to and including the Congressional Medal of Honor. He's the only intelligence officer I ever heard of who got a commendation for shooting up coconut trees.[75]

Richard Rovere noted that as the war years receded, McCarthy's war record grew ever more impressive.

> Running for the Senate in 1944, he said he had been on fourteen missions. In the Senate, in 1948, he claimed seventeen. In 1951, he made it thirty. In 1951 he asked for and in 1952 was given the Distinguished Flying Cross, which is awarded for twenty-five combat missions.[76]

In those postwar years, McCarthy would explain that if he wore elevator shoes (though he was almost six feet tall), "it's because I carry 10 pounds of shrapnel in this leg!"[77] Anderson and May could not resist pointing out that it was impossible to carry this much shrapnel in one leg—all the more so if one had not been wounded in the first place.

But such revelations would come much later. During the war, McCarthy could not have been blamed for feeling that things were going his way.

> In the middle of the third war year, 1944, Captain Joe McCarthy sat back and counted his blessings. He had a record of active duty in the South Pacific; he had made $42,000 on the stock market; and he had kept stories about his war career humming through the printing presses of the Wisconsin newspapers.[78]

Now, he emblazoned the backs of two trucks and a jeep with "MCCARTHY FOR U.S. SENATOR," and across his tent he painted "HEADQUARTERS, MCCARTHY FOR U.S. SENATOR." He had decided to challenge Senator Alexander Wiley in the 1944 Republican primary.

No one knows just when McCarthy became a Republican (his judicial race had been nonpartisan), but there were some Republicans who felt that the conversion was suspiciously sudden, and that McCarthy actually was running a pro-FDR campaign against Wiley. And though the Wisconsin constitution explicitly barred running for partisan office while holding a judicial post, McCarthy simply ignored this technicality.

The campaign was run by a handful of friends and relatives and probably financed (illegally) out of Joe McCarthy's stock-market profits. At the right psychological moment, McCarthy himself arrived, in uniform and with a thirty-day pass. Although military rules prohibited him from making political statements, McCarthy simply prefaced each campaign speech with "If I weren't in military uniform, I would say . . ." and then proceeded to say what he wanted to say. Wiley was renominated, but McCarthy ran second in a field of four, garnering 80,000 votes, which was considered respectable.[79]

In October 1944, McCarthy again requested leave (this time for sixty days), but it was not granted. When leave was denied, McCarthy resigned his commission and was discharged in February 1945. The war was still on, but McCarthy's attentions had turned to the Senate seat held by Robert La Follette, Jr. Returning to Shawano, McCarthy immediately began a round of speechmaking before local clubs, church groups, and bar associations. In 1945, he was easily reelected circuit judge, and began planning for the 1946 Republican Senate primary.

McCarthy's base for his senatorial campaign was to be the state's Young Republicans, but even with such support, McCarthy's chances of winning the Senate seat were held to be virtually nil. To win the Republican nomination, he would almost certainly first need the endorsement of the Republican Voluntary Committee—the chief vehicle for the conservative Stalwart faction that fought the La Follette influence in Wisconsin. La Follette had bolted the GOP in 1934, running as a Progressive in that election and again in 1940. But now, in 1946, he had decided to move back into the Republican party, and the Stalwarts needed a candidate to defeat him.

The dominant leader within the Stalwart faction was Tom Coleman, a wealthy industrialist whose hatred for the La Follettes was legendary. Coleman was desperate to find a candidate who could beat the younger La Follette, but he was at best lukewarm about Joe McCarthy, who did not seem to him a likely winner. Characteristically, McCarthy did not worry about such powerful opposition, however. He merely began running with all the energy at his command.

On the eve of the RVC convention, McCarthy sent a dozen delegates to engage his likeliest challenger, former governor Julius Heil, in small talk. Each delegate told Heil that while Heil had *his* vote, the nomination already appeared locked up for McCarthy. Rather than risk a humiliating defeat in the convention, Heil refused to allow his name to be put into nomination. Earlier, another potentially powerful opponent, Walter Kohler, Jr., had dropped out of the race after a mysterious meeting with McCarthy. It has been suggested that McCarthy threatened to use Kohler's recent divorce against him, although Kohler later forcefully denied this.[80]

In the end, Tom Coleman had little choice but to go along with the endorsement of McCarthy, particularly when McCarthy threatened to run in the primary with or without RVC endorsement. The thought of splitting the anti–La Follette vote and allowing the senator to breeze to renomination was more than Coleman could bear. The RVC endorsement was McCarthy's, and despite a last-minute flap brought about by his refusal to resign his judgeship before beginning a campaign for partisan office, he was on his way to a head-to-head challenge with the symbol of Wisconsin Progressivism.

Wisconsin was quickly buried under an avalanche of direct mailings for McCarthy, and McCarthy himself displayed his usual energy in campaigning, crisscrossing the state, shaking hands and slapping backs wherever he went. Attacking La Follette for his support of the New Deal, for his isolationism, and for having made large profits during the war from his part ownership of a radio station, McCarthy took the offensive. La Follette refused to answer such charges and turned down McCarthy's challenge to debate. A serious, hardworking senator, La Follette preferred to remain in Washington, working on his Legislative Reorganization Act. Capitalizing on La Follette's failure to mend his home fences in recent years, and outspending him $50,000 to $4,000, McCarthy scored something of an upset, defeating the incumbent senator by 5,500 votes (208,000 to 202,500).[81]

The November election would prove to be a mere formality, as McCarthy crushed his Democratic opponent 620,000 to 380,000. He thereby became part of the conservative Republican "Class of 1946," part of the tide that was beginning to turn against the New Deal. For McCarthy himself, of course, his victory was an enormous personal triumph. Just as he had leaped in six years from a grocery store counter to a law office, he had risen in just seven more years from an obscure rural judgeship to the United States Senate. What might he not accomplish in another seven or eight years?

### Senate Career

I lived on a farm for quite some time. . . . The skunks used to come from the woods and kill the baby chicks, steal the eggs, and in general disrupt the operation of the farm.

A group of us used to have to dig out the skunks. . . . It could not be done by passing a resolution against skunks. The nice little boys could pass a resolution against skunks, but the nice little boys did not help us dig them out. It was an unpleasant task; and sometimes after we got through, we were not too welcome sitting next to our friends in church.[82]

Joseph McCarthy arrived in Washington on a December day in 1946. On his first day, he tried to make an appointment with President Truman and was politely turned down. On his second day, he called a press conference to propose that the president end the coal strike by drafting John L. Lewis and the coal miners. Such brashness earned attention, and one of the first magazine articles written about the Wisconsin senator dubbed him a "Remarkable Upstart."[83]

McCarthy quickly proved that he would not be a silent and deferential freshman senator, working diligently to carve out some sphere of personal expertise.

> The observance of Senate folkways requires patience, restraint, and moderation . . . these were qualities the junior senator from Wisconsin singularly lacked. Instead, he brought to the Upper Chamber a restless and compulsive energy, a hunger for power and public notice, and a casual disregard for custom and authority.[84]

His continual violation of Senate norms, rather than any particular stance on policy, was what brought him notoriety. "It didn't take long for McCarthy to establish himself as an arrogant and wildly unpredictable colleague," reports one biographer.[85]

In his first two years in the Senate, McCarthy became prominent in fights to end wartime sugar controls, and to stress prefabricated homes rather than public housing programs. His ties to lobbyists for such measures earned him the nickname the "Pepsi-Cola Kid," and brought him a ten-thousand-dollar fee for writing a short pamphlet opposing public housing. More significant, however, was the manner in which McCarthy conducted himself during these legislative battles.

He showed little regard for the truth, freely manipulated evidence, presented meaningless statistics, misquoted sources, and launched vicious attacks upon those who challenged him. McCarthy was quickly developing a reputation as a troublemaker.

> He had no respect for the spirit of senatorial courtesy or for the rules of seniority, and he was perfectly willing to make personal attacks on fellow senators. The normal social pressures through which the Senate imposes conformity on its members seemed to have little effect on McCarthy.[86]

McCarthy had been marked as a renegade by his behavior, and the mills of Senate justice began to grind. When the Democrats regained control of the Senate in 1949, McCarthy was dropped from the Banking and Currency Committee (at the insistence of its chairman), and the Republican leadership did not lift a finger on his behalf. After but two years in the Senate, McCarthy was already close to being a cipher.

"Get their attention" had been the lesson McCarthy had learned at Marquette, and he began searching for a way to accomplish this. Almost inevitably, he turned to the idea of an investigation, for unlike the legislative process, which was severely circumscribed by formal rules and by the need for cooperation and compromise, the investigative process was steeped in ambiguity. To a great extent when it came to investigations, it was every senator for himself.

Possibly because he believed it might help him with some of his German constituents, McCarthy soon became involved in the investigation of the 1944 Malmédy Massacre. A Senate committee chaired by Raymond Baldwin, a Connecticut Republican, was looking into charges that the confessions of several SS troopers to the murder of a hundred American soldiers at Malmédy had been extracted by torture. Baldwin had routinely encouraged all of his colleagues to participate in the hearings, but only McCarthy took him up on the offer. When McCarthy proposed a list of witnesses and asked to be allowed to cross-examine those called by the subcommittee, Baldwin agreed, perhaps not realizing just what he was letting himself in for.

Before long, McCarthy was dominating the hearings. With a mixture of vituperation, bullying of witnesses, inflated language, and misrepresentation of facts, McCarthy "turned almost every session into a barroom brawl."[87] Richard Rovere recalled how at one point, McCarthy tried to prove the truth of his charges by showing him page after page filled with unconnected facts. The correspondent felt foolish about not seeing the connections, and finally admitted to McCarthy that he did not understand the "evidence." McCarthy explained:

Of course you don't. Naturally they're going to make out the best case they can for themselves. You wouldn't expect them to spill the beans in their own records, would you? The whole thing is a pack of lies.[88]

Still, what mattered most was that attention was being paid. McCarthy drew considerable press coverage from this episode, and as a bonus, Baldwin left the Senate to accept a state judgeship, freely acknowledging that McCarthy's harassment had been the major factor in his decision. The lesson must have been clear once again: Harsh personal attacks with no quarter given were the most effective way of dealing with one's foes, for they would almost invariably lack the inner fortitude to fight back.

As 1950 dawned, Joe McCarthy found himself detested by powerful senators in both parties, under investigation by Wisconsin's tax department, nearly disbarred, and without a major committee assignment. With a reelection campaign coming up in 1952, McCarthy desperately needed a popular issue. Versions differ as to how he came to the issue of domestic Communism and subversion in the government. One oft-told story has it that friends at a Washington lunch proposed various issues (most of them—like the St. Lawrence Seaway—dismissed as unexciting), but that the issue of Communism, suggested by Father Edmund Walsh of Georgetown University, struck a spark. "That's it," McCarthy is supposed to have responded. "The government is full of Communists. We can hammer away at them."[89]

More recent scholarship, however, has cast doubt upon this story. It has been shown, for example, that McCarthy had derived considerable political advantage from successfully employing charges of Communism against a Madison reporter, Cedric Parker of the *Capital Times.* And this had occurred in November 1949, three months before the famous lunch where Father Walsh supposedly handed McCarthy the Communist issue.[90] The success of the attack on Cedric Parker in garnering publicity for McCarthy and in helping him to put his opponents on the defensive seems a more likely source of the impetus that allowed McCarthy's political style to intersect so neatly with the rising arc of fear of Communism in the United States.

Thus, in February 1950, McCarthy flew to Wheeling, West Virginia, for a Lincoln's Birthday address that would tackle the question of Communists in government. It turned out to be a speech that spawned considerable confusion, especially because McCarthy later altered and amended his charges in various ways.[91] He had expected his speech to reach his Wisconsin constituents and to boost his political stock there, but he was quite unprepared to find himself a national figure actually expected to document his charges. Indeed, he had not even kept the materials upon which his charges were based; consequently, not even *he* could be sure of exactly what he had said in Wheeling. But all of this turned out to matter very little compared to the very fact of having won national attention. That the issue of Communists in government could bring such recognition was not to be ignored, and all of McCarthy's skills for self-dramatization were pressed into the service of maintaining this newly won fame.

In the years that followed, McCarthy became embroiled in controversy after controversy. He had hit a raw nerve with some segment of the American public, and his lack of hard evidence did not do much to dim his appeal.

> He had gained an audience, and from the audience came, very rapidly, a following, and from the following came several things of value—increased support within the party, fear of his retaliatory power, nourishment for his strange ego, and money.[92]

McCarthy charged Owen Lattimore, a Johns Hopkins University professor, with being "the top Russian espionage agent in the United States"; blocked the nomination of Philip Jessup as a UN delegate; accused

General George Marshall of being a man who "would sell his grandmother for any advantage"; and became involved in a number of controversies regarding subversion within the U.S. government.

Students of the McCarthy era have concluded that his Senate speech defending his charges at Wheeling was "one of the most fantastic and supremely dishonest performances witnessed on Capitol Hill," and that when McCarthy first spoke of the "top Russian espionage agent," he "hadn't the slightest notion which unfortunate name on his list he would single out for this distinction."[93] *Collier's* thought it "incredible that any American who is both sane and honest can believe that George Marshall or Dean Acheson is a traitorous hireling of the Kremlin."[94] Yet none of this seemed to matter very much, as McCarthy continued to plow forward.

In the 1950 elections, four Democratic senators (including Millard Tydings of Maryland, whom even FDR had been unable to "purge") were defeated for reelection. Despite evidence to the contrary, McCarthy was given credit in Washington for some of these defeats and for Republican victories in some other states. Suddenly, McCarthy, who had been held at arm's length by the Republican leadership, seemed a potentially powerful instrument for helping to end twenty years of Democratic control of the presidency. The "Communist issue" was catching on, and even so respectable a senator as Robert Taft was telling the Wisconsin senator that he should "keep talking and if one case doesn't work out he should proceed with another."[95] Blending his special talents for coaxing maximum publicity from every charge with the willingness of his opponents to respond to every charge, McCarthy seemed to grow increasingly more powerful as time passed.

> Each "startling disclosure" would set in motion a chain of denials, countercharges, corrections, and explanations. Seldom has a politician received so much free advertisement as McCarthy.[96]

Along the way, McCarthy ran into some challenges to his accusations and his tactics, and the history of McCarthyism is, in some sense, also a history of Senate committee investigations. In 1950, the Tydings Subcommittee investigated McCarthy's charges of Communist infiltration of the State Department, and labeled them a "fraud and a hoax." The Gillette Subcommittee investigated McCarthy's role in the 1950 defeat of Senator Tydings and the Wisconsin senator's personal finances. It ended up not only questioning McCarthy's financial ethics, but charging him with "contempt and disdain" for the Senate and the subcommittee. But again, none of this seemed to matter much, especially after the Republicans regained control of the Senate in the 1952 elections.

With Eisenhower in the presidency and Republicans controlling the

Congress, the expectation was that McCarthy would now be brought under control. Passing over McCarthy, the Republican leadership tried to turn the Communist issue over to Senator William Jenner of Indiana by installing him as chairman of the Internal Security Subcommittee and relegating McCarthy to the chairmanship of the relatively unimportant Government Operations Committee. Indeed, McCarthy himself hinted that he would now be turning his attention to graft and corruption. "We've got Joe where he can't do any harm," boasted Majority Leader Robert Taft.[97]

But within two months, McCarthy declared that he had not retired from Communist hunting. There followed a probe of the Voice of America, a tour of Europe by aides Roy Cohn and David Schine (to ferret out supposed subversion in America's overseas libraries), the beginnings of an investigation of various journalists, a one-day hearing that dealt with an alleged "assassination plot" against the senator, and a proposal (quickly dropped) to investigate Communist infiltration of the CIA. By the end of 1953, many found this all beginning to wear a bit thin. Republicans especially began to wonder whose side McCarthy was on. "Still he pressed on . . . driven by some distorted picture of himself and unable to release the whirling merry-go-round of politics and publicity."[98]

Inevitably, attacks on the Eisenhower administration became more frequent, especially after David Schine was drafted and failed to receive sufficiently favorable treatment from the Army. Soon, a probe of Communist infiltration of the Army was underway, with the Army countercharging that McCarthy had sought to pressure the Army on behalf of Schine. What came to be known as the Army-McCarthy hearings began in the late spring of 1954, and many felt that McCarthy's performance in these hearings destroyed him forever. The same tactics that had worked so well for more than four years—vilification, misrepresentation, diversion—seemed suddenly beyond the pale. McCarthy had finally gone too far, or perhaps the definition of boundaries had changed with Republicans in control.[99] Shortly after the Army-McCarthy hearings, a coalition of Democrats and Republicans curbed McCarthy's power as chair of the Government Operations Committee.

The next act was not long in coming, for Senator Ralph Flanders, a Vermont Republican, filed a resolution calling for the censure of Senator McCarthy. A special committee headed by Senator Arthur Watkins, a Utah Republican, was appointed to investigate the charges against McCarthy. The past was now beginning to catch up with the Wisconsin senator. His contemptuous behavior before the 1951 Gillette Subcommittee was exhumed, and his refusal to testify before that body was condemned. This refusal and McCarthy's abuse of General Ralph Zwicker in a 1953 hearing formed the basis of the Watkins Committee's recommendation that censure be voted. The Senate ultimately dropped the Zwicker charge, but added a new one—McCarthy's contemptuous remarks about the Watkins Committee itself. On 2 December 1954, Senator Joseph McCarthy was formally censured by a vote of 67 to 22 in the U.S. Senate.[100]

Five days after the censure vote, McCarthy publicly apologized to the American people for his 1952 support of Dwight Eisenhower for president. Though this caused some consternation among his supporters, it hardly mattered, for when the new Congress reconvened in January 1955, the Democrats were once more the majority, and McCarthy was a forgotten man. No one would even bother to debate him on the Senate floor, and he was largely ignored by all but his few staunch supporters. Colleagues would wander off the floor when McCarthy began to speak, and would even avoid personal contacts. The press no longer reported his speeches, perhaps because they were no longer deemed newsworthy, or perhaps because of a conscious decision to create an informal press blackout.

In 1955 a "McCarthy Day" celebration in Boscobel, Wisconsin, drew only 1,500 (most of them high school marching band members) where 50,000 had been predicted by town leaders. A "comeback address" in Boston was marked by thousands of empty seats. On one occasion, McCarthy was asked to leave a Milwaukee hotel where a campaign dinner for Richard Nixon was in progress. In 1956, every senator but Joe McCarthy was invited to a dinner dance at the White House.[101]

McCarthy was becoming caught up in what has been called "a kind of interior collapse."[102] By 1954, he had already become a full-fledged alcoholic. By the summer of 1956, the problem was so severe that McCarthy began to be hospitalized periodically for detoxification. There were times when he appeared to be in a virtual trance and could not recognize familiar faces. In 1957, McCarthy's investment in a uranium mine went sour, and he lost most of his life savings. Even the adoption of a five-week-old baby girl in January 1957 could not save McCarthy. He died in Bethesda Naval Hospital on 2 May 1957. The motto on McCarthy's office wall had read:

Oh God, don't let me weaken. Help me to continue on. And when I go down, let me go down like an oak tree felled by a woodsman's ax.[103]

Joe McCarthy's political style had deprived him of even that final dignity.

### Notes

1. Oshinsky, *Conspiracy So Immense,* p. 3.
2. Anderson and May, *McCarthy,* p. 7.
3. Ibid., chaps. 2–3.

4. Michael O'Brien, *McCarthy and McCarthyism in Wisconsin* (Columbia: University of Missouri Press, 1980), pp. 1–5; Reeves, *Life and Times*, chap. 1; Oshinsky, *Conspiracy So Immense*, pp. 2–8.

5. O'Brien, *McCarthyism in Wisconsin*, pp. 4–5.

6. Anderson and May, *McCarthy*, p. 7.

7. Cohn, *McCarthy*, p. 12.

8. Eric F. Goldman, *The Crucial Decade—And After: America, 1945–1960* (New York: Vintage Books, 1960), p. 138.

9. Cohn, *McCarthy*, p. 12.

10. Anderson and May, *McCarthy*, pp. 8–9.

11. Rovere, *Senator Joe McCarthy*, p. 78.

12. Anderson and May, *McCarthy*, p. 9.

13. Ibid.

14. Ibid., p. 10.

15. Ibid., p. 11.

16. Ibid.

17. Ibid., p. 12. Oshinsky talked to townspeople who found this story laughable, given Bid McCarthy's deathly fear of machines (see *Conspiracy So Immense*, p. 7).

18. Rovere, *Senator Joe McCarthy*, p. 81.

19. O'Brien, *McCarthyism in Wisconsin*, p. 4.

20. Reeves, *Life and Times*, p. 4.

21. Oshinsky, *Conspiracy So Immense*, pp. 4, 8.

22. Reeves, *Life and Times*, p. 3.

23. Ibid., p. 6.

24. Oshinsky, *Conspiracy So Immense*, pp. 4, 5.

25. Ibid., p. 6.

26. Ibid., p. 8. (emphasis in original).

27. Robert Griffith, "The Notorious Baiter," *Progressive* (November 1982): 57.

28. Greenstein, *Personality and Politics*, pp. 65–66.

29. Oshinsky, *Conspiracy So Immense*, p. 8.

30. Ibid. O'Brien, *McCarthyism in Wisconsin*, suggests that "not enough is known about the child-rearing practices of Joe McCarthy's parents, peer influences, or the progress of his emotional and intellectual growth" (p. 4.).

31. Barber, "Predicting Presidential Styles, p. 61.

32. Ibid., p. 52.

33. O'Brien, *McCarthyism in Wisconsin*, p. 5.

34. Anderson and May, *McCarthy*, p. 15.

35. Ibid., p. 16.

36. Ibid., p. 14.

37. Reeves, *Life and Times*, p. 6.

38. Ibid.

39. Anderson and May, *McCarthy*, pp. 14–15.

40. Oshinsky, *Conspiracy So Immense*, p. 10.

41. Anderson and May, *McCarthy*, pp. 20–21.

42. Ibid., p. 20.

43. Oshinsky, *Conspiracy So Immense*, p. 14.

44. Anderson and May, *McCarthy*, pp. 21–22.

45. Ibid., p. 23.

46. Ibid., p. 19. But compare to Oshinsky's version, *Conspiracy So Immense*, p. 10.

47. Anderson and May, *McCarthy*, p. 23.

48. Oshinsky, *Conspiracy So Immense*, p. 13.

49. Anderson and May, *McCarthy*, p. 24.

50. Cohn, *McCarthy*, pp. 13–14.

51. Reeves, *Life and Times*, p. 18.

52. Anderson and May, *McCarthy*, p. 26.

53. Ibid.

54. Ibid., p. 27. See also O'Brien, *McCarthyism in Wisconsin*, p. 12.

55. Oshinsky, *Conspiracy So Immense,* p. 14.

56. Anderson and May, *McCarthy,* p. 27. This version has McCarthy that day, over a steaming sink at his part-time dishwashing job, deciding on a political career. Reeves, *Life and Times,* pp. 17, 18, claims that there is no evidence in McCarthy's early life of any such political ambition.

57. Anderson and May, *McCarthy,* p. 28.

58. Ibid., p. 30.

59. O'Brien, *McCarthyism in Wisconsin,* p. 17.

60. Reeves, *Life and Times,* p. 22.

61. Oshinksy, *Conspiracy So Immense,* p. 16. O'Brien, p. 23, cites assertions by Waupaca attorneys that McCarthy was almost literally an ambulance chaser.

62. Anderson and May, *McCarthy,* p. 32.

63. Ibid., p. 34.

64. Robert Griffith, *The Politics of Fear: Joseph R. McCarthy and the Senate* (Lexington: University of Kentucky Press, 1970), p. 3.

65. Reeves, *Life and Times,* p. 23.

66. Anderson and May, *McCarthy,* pp. 37–38, suggest that Mike Eberlein had intended to run for this judgeship and was so furious that he ousted McCarthy from the firm. O'Brien, *McCarthyism in Wisconsin,* p. 26, casts considerable doubt upon that version.

67. Anderson and May, *McCarthy,* pp. 39–40.

68. Rovere, *Senator Joe McCarthy,* p. 87.

69. O'Brien, *McCarthyism in Wisconsin,* p. 31, suggests that the matter was not quite so clear-cut. Both the Martindale-Hubbell Law Directory and a forty-year-old Shawano newspaper clipping, though presumably in error, did give the older birthdate for Judge Werner.

70. Anderson and May, *McCarthy,* p. 45.

71. Ibid., pp. 44–45; O'Brien, *McCarthyism in Wisconsin,* pp. 32–33; Oshinsky, *Conspiracy so Immense,* pp. 24–25; Reeves, *Life and Times,* p. 35. The last three, however, suggest that McCarthy's overall record as a judge was not so unrelievedly awful as Anderson and May suggested.

72. O'Brien, *McCarthyism in Wisconsin,* p. 39.

73. Anderson and May, *McCarthy,* pp. 53–54; O'Brien, *McCarthyism in Wisconsin,* p. 43; Reeves, *Life and Times,* p. 42; Oshinsky, *Conspiracy So Immense,* p. 30.

74. Anderson and May, *McCarthy,* pp. 62–65; Reeves, *Life and Times,* pp. 47–49.

75. Anderson and May, *McCarthy,* p. 64.

76. Rovere, *Senator Joe McCarthy,* p. 95.

77. Anderson and May, *McCarthy,* p. 66. O'Brien, *McCarthyism in Wisconsin,* p. 47, suggests that this was a flippant response given by McCarthy, not intended to be taken seriously.

78. Anderson and May, *McCarthy,* p. 67. For McCarthy's war years, see also Reeves, *Life and Times,* pp. 45–54; and Oshinsky, *Conspiracy So Immense,* pp. 30–33.

79. For the 1944 primary campaign, see O'Brien, *McCarthyism in Wisconsin,* pp. 50–53; Reeves, *Life and Times,* pp. 55–59; and Oshinsky, *Conspiracy So Immense,* pp. 34–35.

80. McCarthy's bid for the 1946 RVC Senate race endorsement is described in O'Brien, *McCarthyism in Wisconsin,* pp. 55–62. For the Kohler confrontation, see pp. 61, 221 (n. 26).

81. The 1946 Senate primary is covered in O'Brien, *McCarthyism in Wisconsin,* pp. 62–74. Special attention is given to the famous question of whether Communist votes were crucial to McCarthy's victory.

82. *Congressional Record,* 83d Cong., 2d sess., 1954, 10:14569. This was one of McCarthy's favorite anecdotes, repeated countless times. See Oshinsky, *Conspiracy So Immense,* p. 207.

83. Jack Alexander, "The Senate's Most Remarkable Upstart," *Saturday Evening Post,* 9 August 1947, pp. 15–17, 52–58.

84. Griffith, *Politics of Fear,* pp. 13–14.

85. Oshinsky, *Conspiracy So Immense,* p. 60.

86. Griffith, *Politics of Fear,* p. 19.

87. Oshinsky, *Conspiracy So Immense,* p. 76.

88. Rovere, *Senator Joe McCarthy,* p. 116.

89. Ibid., p. 123.

90. O'Brien, *McCarthyism in Wisconsin*, pp. 91–97.

91. On the Wheeling speech and its aftermath, see Anderson and May, *McCarthy*, chap. 28; Griffith, *Politics of Fear*, pp. 48–57; Reeves, *Life and Times*, chap. 11; and Oshinsky, *Conspiracy So Immense*, chap. 7.

92. Rovere, *Senator Joe McCarthy*, p. 140.

93. Reeves, *Life and Times*, p. 242; Rovere, *Senator Joe McCarthy*, p. 151.

94. Quoted in Oshinsky, *Conspiracy So Immense*, p. 201.

95. William S. White, *The Taft Story* (New York: Harper and Brothers, 1954), p. 85.

96. Griffith, *Politics of Fear*, p. 106.

97. Oshinsky, *Conspiracy So Immense*, p. 251.

98. Griffith, *Politics of Fear*, p. 217.

99. For the Army-McCarthy hearings, see Michael Straight, *Trail by Television* (Boston: Beacon Press, 1954); Reeves, *Life and Times*, chap. 22; and Oshinsky, *Conspiracy So Immense*, chaps. 28–31.

100. For the Senate censure, see Reeves, *Life and Times*, chap. 23; Oshinsky, *Conspiracy So Immense*, chap. 32.

101. These incidents are related in Oshinsky, *Conspiracy So Immense*, chap. 33.

102. Rovere, *Senator Joe McCarthy*, p. 239.

103. Charles Potter, *Days of Shame* (New York: Coward-McCann, 1965), p. 25.

# 3

# McCarthy's Motivational System

## Assessing McCarthy's Character

In 1930, Harold Lasswell proposed the paradigm that was to guide much of the research into political personality for the next half-century: P = p}d}r. In this well-known formula, *P* is the "political man" whose private motives *(p)* are displaced *(d)* onto public objects, and then rationalized *(r)* in terms of the public interest.[1] From this perspective, it is the private motives of a person that provide the fertile ground in which the seeds of political action are planted. In James David Barber's words, motives are "the springs of political energy."[2]

In another context, Barber preferred to talk in terms of "character"—a person's enduring orientation toward life. As noted in Chapter 1, character could be interpreted as providing "at least a link to, and a reflection of, unconscious needs, ego defenses, and psychodynamics."[3] Thus, character must be one of the main factors underlying behavior. If, as shall be seen in the next chapter, world view (or political belief system) helps to give shape to a person's political style, then character (or motives) provides the underlying energies that give the style its thrust. My emphasis for the moment, therefore, will be upon Joe McCarthy's emotional life, and upon the motives that energized him politically. Put bluntly: What did McCarthy want?

Last chapter's brief biographical sketch of McCarthy suggested a man rather clearly dominated by powerful ambitions, yet also in the grip of considerable insecurity. Indeed, one might easily conclude that not much more need be said about McCarthy than that he is an example of Lasswell's "power seeker":

Our key hypothesis about the power seeker is that he pursues power as a means of compensation against deprivation. *Power is expected to overcome low estimates of the self,* by changing either the traits of the self or the environment in which it functions.[4]

55

Certainly this does not seem a bad initial assessment of McCarthy. Given the powerful ambitions evident in his rise from that Wisconsin farm to the U.S. Senate, and the doubts and anxieties one glimpses beneath his jovial exterior, one might certainly conclude that "power seeker" says all one really needs to know about McCarthy. And even if, thanks to recent scholarship, McCarthy's mixture of ambition and self-doubt can no longer blithely be attributed to an unhappy childhood, there remains the McCarthy family's low social status—part of an Irish minority, backwoods farmers—to provide a plausible genesis for McCarthy's attitudes and behavior.

Yet the problem turns out to be considerably more complicated than the previous paragraph might suggest, and perhaps the best way to see that complexity is to attempt to place McCarthy within the framework of analysis developed by Barber—a framework that extends and expands upon Lasswell's initial hypothesis of power seeking as compensation.[5] Barber's approach provides an opportunity to assess Joe McCarthy within the relatively broader context of a typology of political personality. It offers the preliminary theory that will allow some initial baseline measurements of McCarthy's political personality and a sense of the extent to which McCarthy does not fully fit within that theory.

James Barber's model of political personality began with the idea that character could best be analyzed as the product of two independent variables: (1) the dimension of activity/passivity, and (2) the dimension of positive/negative affect toward one's political role (or perhaps toward life in general). The crosscutting of these two dimensions yielded a fourfold typology: active-positive (Lawmaker), active-negative (Advertiser), passive-positive (Spectator), and passive-negative (Reluctant).[6]

This typology was particularly attractive in that it offered a logically comprehensive theory: On the basis of two judgments regarding the dimensions used, *any* person could be placed into one category or another. Of course, the mere fact of having placed a person in a category on the basis of the two dimensions did not guarantee that he would actually behave in a certain way. Simply because a person could be *classified* did not mean that the classification necessarily had any particular *diagnostic* power.[7] That connection—between character type and actual behavior—needed to be empirically demonstrated.[8] James Barber's studies of Connecticut freshman legislators and of United States presidents constituted the empirical testing that convinced him that character and behavior (what he termed "style") were indeed linked in persistent patterns.[9]

Four main styles of political behavior now emerged. The active-positive type focused upon substantive accomplishments and was oriented toward rationality. The active-negative type was ambitious, aggressive, power-seeking. The passive-positive type was concerned primarily with being liked and tended to be compliant in his behavior. The passive-negative type was in politics mainly in response to a sense of civic duty and tended to withdraw from conflict, seeking refuge in rules and rituals. Thus, four different character types reflected four types of motives for being in politics and produced four strategies of adaptation (or styles).

Into which of these categories might Joe McCarthy fall? A logical way to begin is to make assessments of McCarthy on the activity/passivity and positive/negative dimensions. This should enable one to decide which of the four character types McCarthy was closest to in his general orientation toward life. The next step, of course, should be to link that character classification to the appropriate style. Thus McCarthy would no longer be inexplicable except in terms of some ad hoc psychoanalytic theory; he would fit comfortably into a broader theory—a terrain already at least partly charted. He would become simply one more example of a general political type already classified and diagnosed.

It is extremely interesting, therefore, to see what happens, when one tries to fit Senator McCarthy into one of Barber's four categories. It becomes immediately clear that McCarthy's character classification does not mesh with his actual stylistic pattern, and it is this basic divergence from Barber's theory that points in the direction of some key questions to be asked about the special nature of McCarthy's political personality. The breakdown of the fourfold typology described above suggests a number of useful clues to pursue.

Superficially, of course, McCarthy fits into the pattern of the active-positive (or Lawmaker) type. From all the available evidence, the Wisconsin senator seems quite clearly to have been an extremely active and

TABLE 2

FOUR PATTERNS OF ADAPTATION

| | | ACTIVITY | |
| | | *Active* | *Passive* |
| --- | --- | --- | --- |
| WILLINGNESS TO RETURN | *Positive* | Lawmakers | Spectators |
| | *Negative* | Advertisers | Reluctants |

Adapted from Barber, *Lawmakers*, p. 20.

energetic individual all his life. All of McCarthy's biographers agree that McCarthy's energy level was extremely high. Reeves reports that, as a child, McCarthy was "aggressive," "ambitious," and even "hyperactive," while brother Stephen remembered him as "always on the move, daring, willing to take chances." Sister Anna Mae recalled that "Joe always wanted to do something big . . . He never kept still. He was always exploding on something."[10] Oshinsky quotes the same sister: "He wanted—something else—something special."[11]

Looking at the dimension of positive/negative affect, one would have to conclude that McCarthy enjoyed his political activities very much—at least up until the time he was censured by the Senate in 1954. Determining whether someone displays positive or negative affect toward his activities (or toward life in general) is certainly, on the whole, more difficult than making judgments about his location on a scale of activity/passivity. But the main criterion to be used in determining the former asks about the subject whether he is "someone who, on the surfaces we can see, gives forth the feeling that he has *fun* in political life."[12] For McCarthy, by and large, the answer must be in the affirmative. He appears to have reveled in his Senate career and the attendant fuss and fury he generated. Senator Arthur Watkins of Utah, for example, thought of McCarthy as "a person delighted with himself," and felt that "the early McCarthy seemed to enjoy his role."[13] And this seems to have been the general perception of McCarthy. If one is to think, therefore, of the active-negative type as being "pessimistic," "skeptical," and "sad,"[14] it is very hard to envision McCarthy in such terms. Outwardly—certainly "on the surfaces we can see"—McCarthy appears to have derived considerable pleasure from his political career up to 1954.[15]

Thus, if McCarthy's activity and his positive affect toward it are to be accepted at face value, he would have to be labeled an active-positive type. There is nothing inherently wrong in such a classification, of course, except that it does violence to our expectations of the behavior associated with this type.

The active-positive character is linked, in Barber's typology, to a style characterized by an "orientation toward productiveness as a value," "an ability to use his styles flexibly," and "an emphasis on rational mastery."[16] But McCarthy's career confronts one instead with the picture of a man brawling his way through a tumultuous decade, maneuvering for headlines, battling his colleagues, and allowing nothing to stand in his way. McCarthy's hunger for news coverage, his hammer-and-tongs approach to political conflict, his violation of Senate norms—all these things call to mind much more the active-negative (Advertiser) type, with his aggressive stance toward the environment. It is the active-negative type who is "ambitious, striving upward, power-seeking," and who "strikes outward, energetically fighting against the forces that threaten him."[17] One is left, therefore, with a rather clear-cut contradiction between McCarthy's character classification and his actual political style.

Nor does it end the matter simply to accept McCarthy as stylistically active-negative and to chalk him up as an exception. A close examination of the active-negative type as described by Barber quickly makes clear that there are a considerable number of points at which McCarthy's style diverges even from other active-negative types; McCarthy is far from being a typical active-negative. The active-negative, for example, had a tendency to "focus anger on a personal enemy."[18] But one of McCarthy's most perceptive biographers was struck precisely by the fact that

> this most successful and menacing of all our apostles of hatred was himself as incapable of true rancor, spite, and animosity as a eunuch is of marriage. He just did not have the equipment for it. He faked it all and could not understand anyone who didn't.[19]

Like the more typical active-negative, McCarthy was certainly aggressive in much of his political behavior, but there appears to have been a different dynamic at work in McCarthy's aggressiveness—one less rooted in personal hostility and anger. Indeed, most of McCarthy's biographers have noted a sharp dichotomy in his public and private roles.

> To the public McCarthy, life was a game in which no quarter was asked and none given. His approach was so primitive, so cynical, so devoid of commitment to any goal but personal success, that few opponents had the will or stomach to fight him on his own terms. After all, who wants to lock horns with someone who obeys no rules and will do anything—absolutely *anything*—to get what he wants?[20]

Yet as the same biographer notes, when the battle was over, a remarkable transformation took place. "In what seemed a pathetic attempt to disown responsibility for his behavior, McCarthy would go out of his way to meet the victim and express heartfelt concern for his welfare."[21] As Senator Paul Douglas once remarked of McCarthy, "He was like a mongrel dog, fawning on you one moment, and the next trying to bite off your leg."[22]

Moreover, it is important to recognize that McCarthy was not a "true believer," fighting for some deeply held cause.[23] Unlike the active-negative Barber describes—one who needs to believe in the justness of his cause and the scurrilousness of his opponents—McCarthy never took himself or his cause too seriously. "Sometimes he mocked his own performance when talking to senators, and thus disarmed them; he was after all, only playing a political game."[24] Indeed, as early as the 1946 Senate campaign, McCarthy "was impugning his opponent's loyalty strictly for its effect on an audience. He meant no particular harm by the tactic; he was warm and friendly to McMurray off stage."[25]

Another clear difference between Joe McCarthy and the prototypical active-negative lies in their differing attitudes toward political power. For the active-negative president, for example, "life is a hard struggle to achieve and hold power,"[26] and politics is seen as "a means of compensating for power deprivations through ambitious striving."[27] McCarthy, on the other hand, seems rather clearly not to have been a power seeker. Indeed, there is very little in McCarthy's history to demonstrate that he was ever primarily motivated by a desire to exercise or hold power. To the contrary, it could be argued that McCarthy, far from seeking power, actually shied from it.

A number of events and circumstances of McCarthy's Senate career point toward the conclusion that power was not his major concern. One must consider, for example, the extent to which McCarthy placed himself, almost blindly, in the hands of his key aide, Roy Cohn (and to a lesser extent, Cohn's colleague, G. David Schine). "When they came upon something good," Rovere noted, "McCarthy would come in for the kill, but as a rule he had to be told by them what to kill."[28] Indeed, a number of students of the McCarthy years are convinced that McCarthy's confrontation with the army—a confrontation that precipitated his downfall—resulted from his unwillingness or inability to confront Cohn on the issue of Schine's military status.

Schine had been drafted into the army, and Cohn was extremely eager to secure a comfortable post for him, preferably in army intelligence. It was Cohn who pushed McCarthy to take on the army on Schine's behalf. At least some observers are convinced that McCarthy was quite happy to be rid of Schine, but that he was afraid to state this view forthrightly in Cohn's presence.[29]

In addition, Rovere has suggested that, at the end, McCarthy's refusal to compromise on the question of his censure (a refusal that virtually guaranteed that there would be a substantial Republican vote for censure) stemmed not from any rigid moral stand or even from a deep-seated need to fight. Rather, Rovere suggests, McCarthy merely wanted to avoid hurting the feelings of his allies, Senators William Jenner and Herman Welker, who genuinely believed in McCarthy's "mission," and who had labored day and night for the Wisconsin senator's vindication.[30] Thus, far from deriving any inherent satisfaction from dominating others, McCarthy turned out to be the sort of man who

> was unable to hurt anyone's feelings by telling him he didn't want to speak to him on the telephone. Instead of instructing . . . his secretary to tell an unwelcome caller he wasn't in or wouldn't be available for the call, McCarthy would fabricate a long explanation.[31]

Unlike the domineering, power-conscious active-negative type seen in Barber's discussion of Woodrow Wilson and Lyndon Johnson, McCarthy seems to have been quite willing to settle for rewards other than power.

A corollary to McCarthy's lack of concern with exercising power was his minimal concern with organizing for power. As Will Herberg noted, in analyzing the senator's lack of attention to building an organized McCarthyite movement, "Observers have been puzzled by his apparent neglect of these essentials. He has no machine, no party, no press, no agitators, no organization-builders, and he doesn't seem to want any."[32] Examining this aspect of McCarthy's style, Rovere concluded:

> I doubt very much if power—in the sense of office, authority, control—seemed terribly important to him. He revealed no lust or greed for power; he never seemed—to me at least—to be consciously moving toward the American summit, the Presidency. What he lusted for was glory.[33]

One final point of divergence between McCarthy and the active-negative type can be seen in the striking circumstances of the Wisconsin senator's "inner collapse" after he was censured in 1954. Why, after all, should McCarthy have given up so easily after the Senate voted against him? Rovere doubted that the Army-McCarthy hearings and Senate censure were enough, by themselves, to explain McCarthy's political demise.

> There has never been any evidence to suggest that his behavior at the Army-McCarthy hearings lost him any of his real followers. . . . Had he had any real desire to rally them after his 1954 defeats, had he had any organization or any plan for organization, he could have continued as a power in American politics. He might have lost his Senate seat in 1958. But that was four years off and, besides, what demagogue needs a Senate seat?[34]

But "McCarthy took it lying down."[35] It is an odd thing for a powerful demagogic leader (one only in his mid-forties, at that) to surrender so meekly to what were, after all, the mere words of the United States Senate. Yet within a year or two, asked to leave a campaign dinner for Richard Nixon, McCarthy went outside where a newsman who had followed him "found him sitting in an alley, weeping like a little boy."[36]

Indeed, Will Herberg, writing to discredit the notion that McCarthy was a true Hitlerian threat (an article of faith among some liberals), had already noted in 1954 that McCarthy

> has his difficulties and limitations of a kind a genuine Hitler or Lenin, or even a Huey Long would never be confronted with. Imagine Huey Long

vulnerable to a Senate vote of censure, or a Hitler or Stalin dependent on a place in Congress![37]

It is certainly not easy to imagine Barber's active-negative type crumbling quite so easily. One thinks of the active-negative presidents (Hoover, Johnson, Nixon), fighting on and on, past the point of all rationality, to vindicate themselves.

In summary, McCarthy can be seen to diverge from the prototypical active-negative in a number of highly important respects: (1) McCarthy appears to have genuinely emjoyed himself for most of his years in politics. (2) He displayed little genuine, personalized anger against his foes. (3) He required little self-justification for his behavior. (4) He displayed relatively little interest in organizing for, or exercising, power. (5) And at the end, McCarthy surrendered virtually without a struggle.

Despite these evident differences, however, one cannot forget that in much of his outward style, McCarthy did adhere quite closely to the active-negative pattern. He struggled and fought, battled for advancement, and sought publicity and attention. It certainly seems plain that McCarthy was no active-positive seeking a rational approach to public-policy problems; no passive-positive content to watch the spectacle of politics and comply with others' demands; and no passive-negative committed above all to rules and orderly procedures.

And yet he was not quite the active-negative either. He was never one of those "intense young men struggling to prove their power and virtue, working much and laughing little."[38] The questions thus remain: Why did McCarthy not display a negative affect toward his activity? Why did he have no need to create personalized enemies? Why was it unnecessary for him to rationalize his behavior and thereby justify his crusade against domestic Communism. Why did he never display any great love of power? And why, at the end, did he collapse like a pricked balloon? None of these questions can be answered adequately within the framework of the preliminary theory employed here.

## An Analysis of Needs

How can one begin to explain the anomalies uncovered in this study of Joseph McCarthy to this point? Perhaps it makes most sense simply to focus upon the possibility of enhancing the value of the concept of character. In seeking to understand why McCarthy deviated from the ideal type active-negative, perhaps it would be best to examine in detail one element of the overall process of personality development. Specifically, I will focus upon the differences between McCarthy's basic needs and those of the active-negative type.

Left for the next two chapters is an analysis of the extent to which such initial differences are extended and reinforced in the building of the subject's world view. Needless to say, differences in cognitive, moral, and ideological development must constitute another important component of the larger answer to the questions raised by the problem of McCarthy. The remainder of this chapter deals with questions of character. To put the matter another way: If the active-negative is characterized by his struggle for power and virtue, the concern now is with McCarthy's failure to struggle for power. When emphasis is shifted to world view, one can look for explanations for McCarthy's failure to struggle for virtue.

I begin, then, with the concept of character as employed by James David Barber. One of the main criticisms of that concept is that it fails to perform the type of analysis that "specifies the needs the individual seeks to gratify as well as the organizing principle of those needs."[39] Perhaps, therefore, it is by performing precisely that sort of analysis that one may better understand just why McCarthy fails in so many crucial respects to adhere to the model of the active-negative type.

The problem of accommodating an analysis of basic needs into a scheme of personality development immediately raises the question of which particular model of motivation to employ. The entire question of needs, motives, and drives is, needless to say, a highly perplexing one.[40] All one can say with any real degree of certainty is that political psychology will continue to fall short of its lofty goals at least so long as psychology itself can arrive at no consensus on how best to conceptualize and analyze motivation. Yet the advantages of using an explicit theory of motivation seem to outweigh the problems of choosing among so many contenders. In particular, there is the advantage of linking one's findings about such types as the active-negative to some recognized body of psychological thought. One could have far greater confidence in such findings if one were able to believe that they were more firmly grounded in the literature on personality. Secondly, a number of the dynamic processes at work might make a good deal more sense in the context of some established theory of motivation. The nature of the linkage between character and style, for example, might be more understandable given such a framework.[41]

It seems likely, therefore, that analysis of Joseph McCarthy, if it is to be of real use in the long run, must be placed more securely within the framework of some recognized body of psychological thought. Specifically, some unifying theory of motivation and personality, if it could be linked up with the typological approach employed in this study, would offer much hope for future advances in this realm.

In this respect, it may be useful to follow the suggestion of Jeanne Knutson that the "holistic" or "global" perspective of Abraham Maslow is a particularly helpful one for the study of political personality.[42] It is interesting to note, for example, that Maslow's framework for analyzing personality, centering upon his conception of a "hierarchy of needs," has been found useful in a broad range of political studies. These range from examinations of the traditional questions of political philosophy, to the empirical problems of assessing differential effects of varying motivational patterns upon the behavior of political actors, to more wide-ranging analyses of broad macropolitical problems.[43] The advantages to be derived, therefore, from linking the preliminary theory used so far to Maslow's theoretical approach may prove to be considerable in terms of ultimately resolving some crucial problems regarding political personality.

Maslow's basic hypothesis is that people seek to satisfy most those needs they sense to be the most important unsatisfied ones at any given time. Moreover, there exists a set hierarchy of needs applicable to all people, so that one can conceive of a progression from the simplest needs to the most sophisticated. Only as the simplest, most basic needs are satisfied in an individual do his aspirations rise to the satisfaction of more complex needs.

The hierarchy of needs suggested by Maslow consists of five main rungs on a "motivational ladder": (1) the elementary physiological needs (for example, for air, food, water, and sleep); (2) needs for safety and security; (3) "belongingness" and love needs; (4) the need for esteem; and (5) moving beyond the "basic needs" (those which will engender psychic deprivation if they are not satisfied), there is the need for "self-actualization." At this last stage, a person has moved into the realm of the "growth needs," where he seeks satisfaction of his full potentialities and outlets for his genuinely creative energies. He seeks self-fulfillment.[44]

What seems almost immediately evident when one examines the above list of needs is how analogous they seem to the needs that appear to motivate Barber's character types. Ignoring the lowest rung on the motivation ladder—since physiological needs are unlikely to dominate the psyche of any modern American politician—one is left with four main motivations: security, affection, esteem, and self-actualization. One need only turn back to the Reluctant, Spectator, Advertiser, and Lawmaker in order to find a number of very obvious points of comparison with Maslow's framework.

Explicitly adopting the Maslovian model thus gives one the opportunity to test the empirical value of linking a true typology of motivation to the typologies of character and style I have been using so far. The case of Senator McCarthy now offers a good test of the utility of linking the two approaches. Can Maslow's analysis of the esteem seeker (who seems most similar to the active-negative) offer some clues as to why McCarthy does not fit completely the ideal of the active-negative type?

Alexander George, in his lengthy critique of *The Presidential Character* has suggested that its fourfold typology is probably too narrow to capture "the kind of rich developmental and psychodynamic character typology Barber has attempted to formulate."[45] Further differentiation of the basic types is therefore needed in order to develop a richer array of "character subtypes." Maslow's hierarchy of needs offers one immediate reward in this regard, for he divides the esteem seekers into two subtypes. On the one hand, there are those with a need for *self*-esteem, and on the other, those with a need for the esteem of *others*. In Maslow's words:

> These needs may therefore be classified into two subsidiary sets. These are, first, the desire for strength, for achievement, for adequacy, for mastery and competence, for confidence in the face of the world, and for independence and freedom. Second, we have what we may call the desire for reputation or prestige (defining it as respect or esteem from other people), status, fame and glory, dominance, recognition, attention, importance, dignity, or appreciation.[46]

This distinction is muddied by Barber's apparently casual combination of both sets of needs in the character of the Advertiser.

In *The Lawmakers,* Barber's focus seemed to be upon ambition and a desire for advancement as the major driving force in the Advertiser's character. Typically, this type regarded his political career as merely instrumental to his private career needs (law, for example), and saw it as a way of making contacts and generating publicity for himself. The Advertisers were quite open about their purpose, often to the point of cynicism, but Barber viewed this as merely the *conscious* level of motivation. Their *real* motivation, he felt, was the quest for power, for as they moved up the status ladder, they became less subject to others' control and more able to dominate their environment. Power and control were at the heart of their life struggle. The Advertiser in the Connecticut legislature was frequently a lawyer, real estate agent, or insurance man. Such a person was likely to be frustrated by the control that external, political forces were likely to exercise over his life. The rules of his business, for example, would be constantly changing as the result of government activity. Thus, for the Advertiser, the entry into politics would be a way to challenge the domination of politics by becoming one of the dominators. In this way, Barber argued, a strong (but presumably unconscious) drive for power would manifest itself.[47] At the conscious level, however, the Advertiser might well be aware of no more than a powerful desire to advance himself by making contacts and generating publicity.

In *The Presidential Character,* however, the emphasis shifted to a *conscious* power orientation. While the Advertiser had evaluated his behavior in terms of "speeding or slowing his march toward higher positions," the active-negative presidents were quite explicitly "evaluative with respect to power."[48] These presidents were greatly concerned with proving their "strength," and Barber now stated his central hypothesis as follows:

> Having experienced severe deprivations of self-esteem in childhood, the person develops a deep attachment to *achievement* as a way to wring from his environment a sense that he is worthy; progressively, this driving force is translated into a search for independent *power* over others, pursued with intense dedication, and justified idealistically. Whatever style brings success in domination is adopted and rigorously adhered to.[49]

Thus, the focus was now increasingly upon the active-negative type as a power-motivated individual. There is a real question, however, as to the value of such a focus in seeking to understand the complexities of the political personality.[50] Moreover, even in *The Presidential Character,* the active-negative type is described as "ambitious, striving upward, power-seeking,"[51] as though these were essentially equivalent terms. Yet it seems reasonable to assert that ambitious behavior is not always power-seeking behavior. The seeking of political advancement may well be instrumental behavior both for those seeking power and for those seeking "reputation or prestige" (in Maslow's phrase). The surface similarities of such ambitious striving should not conceal the underlying differences of the motivational patterns. Naturally enough, differences in basic needs can produce considerably different behavioral styles. If the active-negative seeks power (as a means of repairing damaged self-esteem), it ought not to be surprising that McCarthy, seeking recognition and attention (as a symbol of the esteem of others), differs notably from the former in many respects.

If one now moves toward understanding McCarthy in terms of a need for recognition and attention, rather than a need for power, much that is incomprehensible or confusing about his behavior (as viewed from Barber's perspective) becomes considerably clearer. Both types may well display aggressive behavior, but while the need for power generates aggression as a tension-reducing mechanism, the need for attention is far likelier to be linked to aggression as an instrumental value. Rather than being genuinely psychically rooted, the latter type of aggression is learned behavior, employed as a tool in striving for ends that are not in and of themselves aggressive. As one example of this,

> a boy may learn that his hostile actions often bring him the attention he desires. He may then come to perform aggressive responses whenever relevant cues (signs of neglect or indifference in important people around him) arouse his desire for attention. The instigating sequence in

this case might be as follows: He responds to the external cues with the thoughts, "No one is paying attention to me. I must get their attention." An "attention motive" is aroused, and this produces the hostility in the presence of suitable "releaser cues," the sight of appropriate people who could give him the attention he wants.[52]

In many ways, this seems a far more suitable description of Joseph McCarthy's aggressive behavior than does the description of psychically based aggression.

A second interesting point raised by George concerns the necessity for moving toward "mixed types" in the analysis of political personality. The creation of such character subtypes as discussed above "will move the typology from pure types into mixed types that will reflect the greater complexity of character in real life."[53] The possibilities for mixed types would appear to flow more readily from a "hierarchy of needs" than from a fourfold table. It becomes far simpler, for example, to conceive of the slow merging of one need, at its upper levels, into the lower levels of the need above it on the motivational ladder. The need for the esteem of others, for example, can be viewed as emerging after satisfaction of needs for affection, while the need for self-esteem can be viewed as just preceding the development for self-actualization needs.[54] In contrast, there is really no logical interrelation to be deduced from among Barber's four categories. No category appears particularly closer to another category than to a third.[55] With Maslow's framework, therefore, one can think in terms of levels that are "interdependent and overlapping, each higher need level emerging before the lower needs have been satisfied completely."[56] Maslow illustrates this point by noting that

> In actual fact, most members of our society who are normal are partially satisfied in all their basic needs and partially unsatisfied in all their basic needs at the same time. A more realistic description of the hierarchy would be in terms of decreasing percentages of satisfaction as we go up the hierarchy of prepotency. For instance, if I may assign arbitrary figures for the sake of illustration, it is as if the average citizen is satisfied perhaps 85 percent in his physiological needs, 70 percent in his safety needs, 50 percent in his love needs, 40 percent in his self-esteem needs, and 10 percent in his self-actualization needs.[57]

This adds a conceptual complexity considerably beyond what one is yet capable of dealing with, but which may help to understand the welter of confusion surrounding any attempt to classify neatly any particular subject. No real person, of course, is motivated entirely by one specific need. Nonetheless, even from the relatively simplified form of Maslow's basic hierarchy, some interesting results can be drawn from the classification of McCarthy as a type motivated by a need for the esteem of others.

If McCarthy is regarded as of a type standing between those motivated by a need for affection and those motivated by a need for self-esteem, this would be, in Barber's terms, equivalent to a type somewhere between the active-negative and the passive-positive.[58] One ought not to be surprised, therefore, that he displayed some qualities peculiar to each. No doubt McCarthy wanted above all to be noticed and paid attention to, but one cannot ignore his gregarious behavior either. "He showed a warmth and a desire to be liked, even by his opponents, which this reporter found touching," one journalist noted during the Army-McCarthy hearings.[59] McCarthy's dilemma can perhaps best be summed up in the same journalist's observation that "he wanted deeply to be liked by everyone, but he would rather be hated than ignored."[60] The tragedy for McCarthy was that the satisfaction of the former need was increasingly precluded by what he did in order to assure that he was not ignored. Recognition and attention came to be valued above all, and it can surprise no one to hear of McCarthy wandering excitedly about the Senate floor during a crucial debate, completely occupied in showing all his colleagues a letter that had reached him with only postage and his photograph affixed.[61] Perhaps Senator Clinton Anderson came closest to the mark in analyzing McCarthy's basic needs when he described how a number of defeats at gin rummy had provoked feverish study of the rules by the Wisconsin senator:

> I attribute the improvement to his discomfort at being so frequently humiliated by his colleagues. I don't think he took any pleasure in playing a better gin rummy game, only in getting some respect and attention from his associates in the Senate.[62]

Maslow's approach, allowing the classification of McCarthy as a seeker of respect and attention, helps also to explain his failure to organize for higher office. As long as McCarthy's immediate need for others' esteem was being met by the press coverage of the ballyhoo he created in the Senate, higher office was unnecessary. Unlike the power-oriented personality who feels closed in or controlled by higher authority, McCarthy was perfectly content to function within his own sphere so long as he had his place in the sun. It is even conceivable that, unlike the power seeker, McCarthy could acknowledge his limitations to himself, and never took himself so seriously as to imagine he would make a very good president. He may have been perfectly content to remain in an office where all he had to do was talk, rather than moving beyond his depth in an office like the presidency. Only after he could no longer activate mass press coverage in the Senate did McCarthy even broach the suggestion to some Republican leaders that he might challenge Eisenhower's renomination in 1956.[63] The idea was never seriously pursued beyond this, and died virtually upon birth. Thus, if the analysis presented so far is correct, one is in a position to suggest that one basis for McCarthy's divergence from the ideal type of the active-negative—demonstrated in his ability to enjoy himself in the Senate, his failure to display personalized anger against his foes, his minimal concern for self-justification, and his ignoring of power opportunities—lies in the different motivational base for his behavior. Since McCarthy was not motivated primarily by a need to compensate for power deprivations, many of the stylistic concomitants of that need were not present in the total pattern of his behavior.

In the end, of course, the results both for America and for McCarthy himself differed considerably from what might have been the case had the Wisconsin senator been genuinely power motivated. For Rovere, McCarthy clearly lusted for glory more than power, and

> the glory drive is always less dangerous, because it is more easily frustrated. It is selfish, or self-seeking, in the narrowest sense, and it makes defeat and humiliation a personal affair. A discouraged politican with no deep sense of mission can go off with reveries of peace into the Arizona desert, but a man possessed could never do so, for he knows that his dreams and demons could not follow him.[64]

McCarthy's inner collapse following the 1954 censure, therefore, is better understood when one understands that he was not driven by the power need and its associated need for the moralization and rationalization of that drive. The active-negative type, seeking power and virtue is unlikely to surrender quite so easily in the face of defeat. It is far easier, however, to break the spirit of a man who relies upon the constant feedback of others' esteem. When the person who desperately needs attention and respect finds that nothing he does brings that attention or respect, his psychic collapse seems virtually inevitable. Without the recognition he needed in order to sustain himself, McCarthy had nothing to fall back upon at the end. So long as his escapades had brought him newspaper headlines, his Senate colleagues had been forced to pay attention whether they liked it or not. After the censure, however, McCarthy found that, apart from his staunchest supporters (Senators Jenner, Welker, and Malone), he was essentially a nonperson. As Senator Arthur Watkins recalled McCarthy's last years,

> There was no concerted effort at all on the part of his Senate colleagues to give him the icy treatment, but increasingly as McCarthy got up on the floor of the Senate to make remarks the other Senators would drift off the floor and find other interests in the cloakroom, or go to the washroom. If a group of Senators stood in the cloakroom enjoying a story and Joe joined them, the laughter quickly faded and the various Senators went on their way.[65]

When he tried to join his colleagues at lunch, they would quickly finish their meals and mumble excuses about having to return to the office. "The merriment had long since disappeared from McCarthy's eyes," recalled Watkins, "and he could be seen watching after his departing colleagues with a look of real puzzlement on his face."[66] His bills were defeated by lopsided margins (one that would have required President Eisenhower to raise the issue of Eastern Europe at a forthcoming summit meeting with the Soviets was defeated 77 to 4), his name was stricken from the White House guest list, and his patronage recommendations were simply ignored.

Worst of all was the attitude of the press. "Joe was deeply hurt by this unspoken policy of the journalists," reports Reeves.[67] McCarthy had thrived upon press coverage, but now

> at the announcement of a McCarthy speech, the reporters in the press gallery would see a chance to catch a bite, to exchange gossip, or to find out what Lyndon Johnson was up to. Handouts from McCarthy's office would land in the wastebaskets, and the group that had called itself "the goon squad"—the dozen or so correspondents who for nearly five years had been assigned to covering his every word—was disbanded.[68]

At one point in 1955, McCarthy offered the *Milwaukee Journal* a copy of a speech in which, claiming to have been influenced by reading Jefferson, he now upheld the right to dissent and to hold unpopular or even subversive beliefs. Even this did not win him press coverage.[69]

With the rewards of recognition and attention denied him, there was nothing for McCarthy to fall back upon—no ideological commitment, no certainty of his moral superiority, not even a true thirst for vengeance. As Rovere summed it up, "McCarthy was finished in 1954 not because he had suffered wounds of a kind no demagogue could survive, but because he had suffered wounds that a particular demagogue named Joseph R. McCarthy could not survive."[70]

Thus, my conclusion is that Joe McCarthy is not completely analyzable within the limits defined by the active-negative type. McCarthy represents a type (or perhaps subtype) not explainable in terms of Barber's fourfold typology, but more likely to be understood when examined in the light of Abraham Maslow's "hierarchy of needs." A number of puzzling characteristics displayed by McCarthy can be more readily comprehended by regarding him, not as a genuinely active-negative type and not as a power seeker, but as a man motivated primarily by a need for the esteem of others. In this way, by harking back to the question of basic needs, particularly as these can be linked to Barber's concept of "character," it becomes possible to develop a systematic approach to understanding the functioning of Joe McCarthy's political personality in its fuller context.

No explanation solely in terms of needs or character, of course, can by itself account for the totality of McCarthy's political behavior. It remains necessary to link the motivational aspects of McCarthy's behavior to such concepts as belief system, moral development, and ideology—the topics of the next two chapters. It is only as one comes to see the particular energies flowing from McCarthy's motivational system being given shape and structure by his particular political belief system that one approaches an understanding of the forces at work in McCarthy's psychic economy.

## Notes

1. Harold D. Lasswell, *Psychopathology and Politics* (1930; reprint, New York: Viking Press, 1960), pp. 74–76.

2. James David Barber, "Adult Identity and Presidential Style: The Rhetorical Emphasis," *Daedalus* 97 (Summer 1968): 950.

3. George, "Assessing Presidential Character," p. 241.

4. Harold D. Lasswell, *Power and Personality* (New York: W. W. Norton, 1948), p. 39 (emphasis in original).

5. James David Barber, *The Lawmakers: Recruitment and Adaptation to Legislative Life* (New Haven: Yale University Press, 1965); idem, "Predicting Presidential Styles," pp. 51–80; idem, "Adult Identity," pp. 938–68; idem, "President and Friends"; idem, *Presidential Character*. Barber presents an interesting description of his research processes in "Strategies of Understanding Politicans," *American Journal of Political Science* 18 (May 1974): 443–67. Critiques of Barber's approach can be found in Erwin Hargrove, "Presidential Personality and Revisionist Views of the Presidency," *American Journal of Political Science* 17 (November 1973): 819–35; George, "Assessing Presidential Character," pp. 234–82; James H. Qualls, "Barber's Typological Analysis of Political Leaders," *American Political Science Review* 71, (March 1977): 182–211; and Michael Nelson, "The Psychological Presidency," in *The Presidency and the Political System,* ed. Michael Nelson (Washington: CQ Press, 1984), pp. 156–78.

6. The nomenclature in terms of dimensions comes from Barber, *Presidential Character.* The terms in parentheses represent the more colorful nomenclature employed in Barber's earlier study, *Lawmakers.*

7. For the distinction between classification and diagnosis, see George, "Dynamic Psychology," p. 80.

8. Greenstein, *Personality and Politics,* pp. 22–23, discusses the idea of linking nuclear and correlational types.

9. Barber, *Lawmakers;* idem, *Presidential Character.*

10. Reeves, *Life and Times,* pp. 4–5. The problem of attempting accurate classification on the basis of nonoperationalized variables should not be underestimated. Hargrove, "Presidential Personality," p. 832, disagrees with Barber's classification of presidents Coolidge and Eisenhower as passive-negative. Both Barber and Hargrove make judgments on the basis of impressionistic analyses of the relevant variables, and these, obviously, always remain open to question.

11. Oshinsky, *Conspiracy So Immense,* p. 6. A numer of McCarthy biographies describe how McCarthy worked anonymously on a North Dakota farm during one Senate recess, trying to burn off excess energy. See, for example, Oshinsky's account, p. 57.

12. Barber, *Presidential Character,* p. 11.

13. Arthur V. Watkins, *Enough Rope* (Englewood Cliffs, N.J.: Prentice-Hall, 1969), pp. 180, 182. Lately Thomas, *When Even Angels Wept* (New York: William Morrow, 1973), p. 98, speaks of McCarthy's "cheerful pugnacity."

14. These descriptors are Barber's; see *Presidential Character,* p. 12. For the correlational

traits associated with the active-positive type, see Barber, *Lawmakers,* pp. 102–4, 216; also idem, *Presidential Character,* pp. 95–98.

15. It is possible, of course, to argue that this positive affect was "superficial," and that beneath the surface McCarthy actually concealed great unhappiness about the nature of his life. However, Barber's passive-positive (Spectator) type is considered by him to display positive affect even though he explicitly refers to this type's "superficial optimism" ("President and Friends," p. 12).

16. Barber, *Presidential Character,* p. 12.

17. Ibid. See also Barber, *Lawmakers,* p. 215.

18. Barber, *Presidential Character,* p. 97. Similarly, Lasswell's agitator "easily infers that he who disagrees with him is in communion with the devil, and that opponents show bad faith or timidity" (*Psychopathology and Politics,* p. 78).

19. Rovere, *Senator Joe McCarthy,* p. 59.

20. Oshinsky, *Conspiracy So Immense,* pp. 14–15.

21. Ibid., p. 15. Among those who found themselves in similar situations were Senator Ralph Flanders (Rovere, *Senator Joe McCarthy,* pp. 54–55); Dean Acheson (Thomas, *When Even Angels Wept,* p. 237); and Senator Robert Hendrickson (Cook, *Nightmare Decade,* p. 76).

22. Paul H. Douglas, *In The Fullness of Time* (New York: Harcourt Brace Jovanovich, 1972), p. 251.

23. See the more extensive discussion of this issue in Chapter 4 below.

24. Harry McPherson, *A Political Education* (Boston: Little, Brown, 1972), p. 78.

25. Reeves, *Life and Times,* p. 103.

26. Barber, *Presidential Character,* p. 12.

27. Barber, "President and Friends," p. 12.

28. Rovere, *Senator Joe McCarthy,* p. 195.

29. Oshinsky, *Conspiracy So Immense,* pp. 438–40. See also Potter, *Days of Shame,* pp. 24–34, 38–44.

30. Rovere, *Senator Joe McCarthy,* pp. 56–57.

31. Cohn, *McCarthy,* p. 267. Another incident recounted by Cohn has McCarthy giving a good story to a hostile reporter because, after all, "he's got to make a living" (p. 268).

32. Will Herberg, "McCarthy and Hitler: A Delusive Parallel," *New Republic,* 23 August 1954, p. 15.

33. Rovere, *Senator Joe McCarthy,* pp. 46–47. "He never organized, even in the simplest way," Rovere concludes (p. 143). See also Cohn, *McCarthy,* p. 248.

34. Richard Rovere, "McCarthy: As National Demagogue," in *The Meaning of McCarthyism,* 2d ed., ed. Earl Latham (Lexington, Mass.: D. C. Heath, 1973), p. 192.

35. Ibid.

36. Oshinsky, *Conspiracy So Immense,* p. 503.

37. Herberg, "McCarthy and Hitler," p. 15. Cohn, *McCarthy,* p. 262, puts it in terms of a loss of "self-respect," and asserts that McCarthy would have regained it had he lived to win renomination and reelection in 1958.

38. Barber, *Presidential Character,* p. 100.

39. Jeanne N. Knutson, "Personality in the Study of Politics," in *Handbook of Political Psychology,* ed. Jeanne N. Knutson (San Francisco: Josey-Bass, 1973), p. 41.

40. A useful discussion of the meaning of motivation can be found in David G. Winter, *The Power Motive* (New York: Free Press, 1973), chap. 2.

41. Daniel Katz, "Patterns of Leadership," in *Handbook of Political Psychology,* p. 231. Katz wonders of Barber's framework "why his two dimensions . . . should generate the properties attributed to his four characters types. . . . These properties derive neither from any logical propositions nor from careful account of the psychodynamic processes assumed."

42. The argument has been discussed at length in Jeanne N. Knutson, *The Human Basis of the Polity* (Chicago: Aldine-Atherton, 1972); idem, "Personality in Politics"; and idem, "Prepolitical Ideologies: The Basis of Political Learning," in *The Politics of Future Citizens,* ed. Richard G. Niemi, (San Francisco: Josey-Bass, 1974).

43. See especially James C. Davies, *Human Nature in Politics* (New York: John Wiley,

1963); Christian Bay, *The Structure of Human Freedom* (Stanford: Stanford University Press, 1958); Stanley Allen Renshon, *Psychological Needs and Political Behavior* (New York: Free Press, 1974); Ronald Inglehart, "The Silent Revolution in Europe: Intergenerational Change in Post-Industrial Societies," *American Political Science Review,* 65 (December 1971): 991–1017; Alan Marsh, "The 'Silent Revolution,' Value Priorities, and the Quality of Life in Britain," *American Political Science Review,* 69 (March 1975): 21–30.

44. The core of Maslow's work on value hierarchies can be found in Abraham H. Maslow, *Motivation and Personality,* 2d ed. (New York: Harper and Row, 1954). Maslow's "Theory of Human Motivation," originally published in the *Psychological Review* in 1943, has been reprinted in *Dominance, Self-Esteem, Self-Actualization: The Germinal Papers of A. H. Maslow,* ed. Richard J. Lowry (Monterey, Calif.: Brooks/Cole, 1973).

45. George, "Assessing Presidential Character," p. 278. Another approach to making finer distinctions would be that proposed by Fred I. Greenstein, "Political Psychology: A Pluralistic Universe," in *Handbook of Political Psychology,* p. 456 n. 1 (a treatment of Barber's dichotomous variables as continuous ones).

46. Maslow, *Motivation and Personality,* p. 45. The listing of "dominance" in the second category does not seem quite right here, but may reflect the extremely complex question of where on the need hierarchy to place "power-motivation."

47. Barber, *Lawmakers,* pp. 231–32.

48. Ibid., p. 89; Barber, *Presidential Character,* p. 96.

49. Barber, *Presidential Character,* p. 100 (emphasis in original).

50. See James L. Payne and Oliver H. Woshinsky, "Incentives for Political Participation," *World Politics* 24 (July 1972): 518–46, for the suggestion that power is basically an instrumental goal, used in attaining other, more valued, ends. James L. Payne, Oliver H. Woshinsky, Eric P. Veblen, William H. Coogan, and Gene E. Bigler, *The Motivation of Politicians* (Chicago: Nelson-Hall, 1984), does not even list *power* in its index.

51. Barber, *Presidential Character,* p. 12. A useful distinction is made in Rufus P. Browning, "The Interaction of Personality and Political System in Decisions to Run for Office: Some Data and a Simulation Technique," *Journal of Social Issues* 24 (July 1968): 93–109. Browning discerns "status-oriented" politicians with low needs for power and high needs for status, and "organization-oriented" politicians with high needs for power.

52. Leonard Berkowitz, *Aggression: A Social Psychological Analysis* (New York: McGraw-Hill, 1962), p. 259.

53. George, "Assessing Presidential Character," p. 278.

54. The suggestion that the need for the esteem of others ranks below the need for self-esteem on the motivational ladder was first made by Maslow in "Theory of Motivation," p. 162 n. 6. Knutson, *Human Basis of Polity,* p. 49, conceptualizes the relationship of the two in the same way on the basis of "generally accepted psychological theory."

55. Thus, Barber finds rather puzzling the tendency of his Advertisers to display some of the Spectator's characteristics from time to time (see *Lawmakers,* pp. 106–7). That tendency becomes a good deal more understandable if one regards the seeker of the esteem of others as located somewhere between those motivated by the need for self-esteem (Advertisers) and those motivated by the need for affection (Spectators).

56. Paul R. Lawrence and John A. Seiler, eds., *Organizational Behavior and Administration,* rev. ed. (Homewood, Ill.: Dorsey Press, 1965), p. 448.

57. Maslow, *Motivation and Personality,* pp. 53–54. "In most persons, a single primary all-important motive is less often found than a combination in varying amounts of *all* motivations working simultaneously" (*Motivation and Personality,* p. 3).

58. See above, note 55.

59. Straight, *Trial by Television,* p. 240. Woodrow Wilson also appears to have been driven by two needs—for power and for affection. Alexander L. George and Juliette L. George, *Woodrow Wilson and Colonel House* (New York: John Day, 1956), p. 319 n, suggest that most of the latter need was satisfied by his family and friends, leaving the political arena for the pursuit of power.

60. Straight, *Trial by Television,* p. 243. Goldston, *American Nightmare,* p. 182, suggests that "in a sense his entire Senate career may be seen as the increasingly desperate attempt of an outcast, a pariah, to establish contact with his fellows."

61. Rovere, *Senator Joe McCarthy,* p. 69.

62. Clinton P. Anderson with Milton Viorst, *Outsider in the Senate: Senator Clinton Anderson's Memoirs* (New York: World Publishing, 1970), p. 102.

63. Feuerlicht, *McCarthy and McCarthyism,* p. 147.

64. Rovere, *Senator Joe McCarthy,* p. 254.

65. Watkins, *Enough Rope,* p. 183.

66. Ibid.

67. Reeves, *Life and Times,* p. 668.

68. Rovere, *Senator Joe McCarthy,* pp. 239–40; also Thomas, *When Even Angels Wept,* pp. 627–28.

69. Edwin R. Bayley, *Joe McCarthy and the Press* (Madison: University of Wisconsin Press, 1981), pp. 217–18.

70. Rovere, *Senator Joe McCarthy,* p. 237.

# 4

## McCarthy's Political Belief System:
## Nature and Functioning

### Political Belief Systems

McCarthy's motivational system was, as seen above, a crucial determinant of his political style. Understanding to some degree the nature of his motivation gives one a sense of the fierce energies underlying the McCarthy era. Here was a man furiously driven to attain the attention and respect of others, and out of those private needs came the pressures that generated Joe McCarthy's behavior in the political arena.

In the previous chapter, therefore, I focused upon the *p* of Harold Lasswell's famous equation—the "private motives" that drive the political man. In this chapter and the next, my emphasis will be upon the way in which McCarthy *displaced* those private motives onto public objects and the way in which he *rationalized* such displacement (or more, accurately, failed to rationalize it).[1]

I turn then from the basic needs generating McCarthy's drives to the channeling of those drives in the particular directions that shaped McCarthy's style. The need for respect from others does not by itself determine one's political style, and one needs therefore to examine McCarthy's attitudes toward "public objects" (for example, the political arena) in order to approach a fuller understanding of his political style.

If it can be said that an individual's basic needs generate within him a particular set of drives, there still remains considerable leeway as to precisely how such drives will ultimately be channeled. The concept of world view, comprising a person's "ideological investments," his "view of social causality," and his "view of human nature," conveys the idea that it is only as one begins to develop some beliefs about how and why the world functions that genuine life choices become possible.[2] It is the possession of a world view—how one perceives and justifies one's place in the political order—that provides some orientation to one's drives and gives one a sense of location in the political world.

Although the theoretical significance of the concept of world view as a basis for the understanding of political personality is clear, there is some difficulty in actually employing it. The almost literary quality of the term leaves it a somewhat fuzzy concept, and makes it harder to link to the terminology more commonly employed in psychological studies.

Alexander George, however, has offered a concrete suggestion for enhancing the conceptual clarity of this basically useful notion. Specifically, he suggests that the analytic limitations of *world view* might well be overcome by substituting for it *belief system,* an idea far more solidly rooted in the generally accepted terminology of political psychology.[3] Milton Rokeach, for example, has defined a belief system as "the beliefs, sets, expectancies, or hypotheses, conscious or unconscious, that a person at a given time accepts as true of the world he lives in."[4]

From this congeries of beliefs, one can then abstract (at least for analytic purposes) the *political* belief system—"the set of beliefs according to which individuals navigate and orient themselves in the sea of politics."[5] Moreover, the concept of belief system has the additional advantage of fostering an analysis of style of belief, as well as content of belief. The more substantive connotations of *world view* do not appear to give sufficient consideration to the importance of *how* beliefs are held as compared to *what* is held.

Yet cognitive style is certainly an important aspect of overall political style, and

> it is by employing the concept of cognitive style, and by working within the framework of the particular cognitive style displayed by the subject, that the investigator can identify and assess the interaction among the psychodynamic patterns, ego defenses, and constructive coping resources available to the individual.[6]

Thus, there is much to occupy one's attention in this realm that lies between motives and style. In the words of one political scientist, between the

> fundamental needs and psychic compulsions, on the one hand, and fairly specific, perhaps transient opinions, on the other, lies a set of orientations toward society and politics that has been less intensively examined. Here we find the beliefs and values and habits of thought that guide and inform a politician's more ephemeral reponses to his environment and that are dependent in ways yet unknown on his deeper personality structure.[7]

In this respect, perhaps Harold Lasswell's views on the centrality of rationalization *(r)* can offer a most useful starting point, for despite the stress laid upon the private motives in most psychohistorical research, that is certainly not the only route to understanding. Indeed, Lasswell reminds us that

> the political man shares the *p,* the private motives which are organized in the early life of the individual, with every man, and the *d,* the displacement on to public objects, with some men. The distinctive mark of the *homo politicus* is the rationalization of the displacement in terms of the public interest.[8]

There may be many who seek power as a way of compensating for childhood deprivations,[9] but only some displace that need upon the public arena, and even fewer seek to rationalize that displacement in terms of the public interest. For two of Lasswell's varieties of political man—the administrator (compulsive character) and the agitator (dramatizing character)—there was indeed a powerful need to be able to justify their power-seeking behavior in terms of some claims of principle or higher values.[10]

The line of analysis suggested by Lasswell was carried forward by Alexander and Juliette George in their study of the "compulsive" aspects of Woodrow Wilson's political behavior.[11] Their position was that Wilson had sought power as a "compensatory value, a means of restoring the self-esteem damaged in childhood," but that "he could indulge his hidden desire to dominate only by 'purifying' his leadership, by committing it to political projects which articulated the highest moral and idealistic aspirations of the people."[12] Again, the importance of rationalization in the psychic economy of the political man was emphasized.

More recently, James David Barber's depiction of the Advertiser, or active-negative type, has followed this path.[13] Though denying that there was only one clear type of political man, Barber did acknowledge that the type sketched by Lasswell was certainly common enough in American politics. Barber's active-negative was indeed driven by low self-estimates and sought to compensate by seeking status and power over others.

Thus, Barber described a politician working to meet his deeper needs by adopting a style aimed at continual advancement and at success in dominating others. But success proved elusive for the active-negative, because as Barber concluded:

> He sets for himself a high standard of achievement; he wants to be great, to accomplish something immortal. But in the course of pursuing his goals he finds himself in morally ambiguous circumstances, threatening to his integrity. The desire to achieve good things is blemished by the necessity of questionable means. The Advertiser feels anxious about his life strategies; he also seems to feel guilty about his tactics.[14]

Measuring himself against two conflicting value scales—a status/power scale ("Am I winning or losing?") and a virtue scale ("Am I being bad or good?")—the active-negative sensed, even if he could not admit it to himself, that in order to succeed, he had compromised his virtue.

The conflict thereby created can thus be seen as generating the need for a rationalization in terms of the public interest. Since few are willing to admit that they are motivated primarily by a concern for themselves at the expense of others, it becomes necessary to create some sort of framework that will enable one to justify one's actions in terms of a greater public good. Despite that structure of rationalization, however, doubts persist.

Thus, there continued to be an inner struggle that the active-negative was never able satisfactorily to resolve. He could not easily compromise with others, for to do so would threaten the sense of high purpose that enabled him to justify his striving behavior. Furthermore, since outsiders might regard political compromise as self-serving, and see it as necessarily stemming from base motives, the active-negative found it necessary to take rigid, unyielding stances. By insisting that he had no choice but to behave as he did—that a moral principle was involved—this type could defend himself against all those who might otherwise be able to accuse him of political expediency.[15]

Thus, it becomes immediately apparent that self-righteousness will necessarily be a major component of the active-negative's personality. He will need to believe deeply in the propriety of his own actions and in the venality of those of his opponents. Without that belief in his own morality, this type would be forced to conclude that at least some of the actions taken in his drive for success violated the standards demanded by his sense of virtue; the results would in all likelihood prove psychologically devastating. Barber's case studies of presidents Wilson, Hoover, Lyndon Johnson, and Nixon offered considerable evidence in support of the contention that the active-negative type tended to be characterized by a high degree of self-righteousness. Such a finding served to reaffirm the significance of rationalization as propounded in Lasswell's formula.

Yet if the work of Lasswell, the Georges, and Barber helps to establish the crucial role of rationalization in the psychic economy of the political man, it also raises some important questions. Specifically, one must wonder whether there have been political leaders who did not have this need to rationalize their behavior. What psychological dynamics would be at work in such a personality? What would the consequences be, both for the politician and for the political environment within which he operated? The case of Senator Joseph McCarthy offers an opportunity to explore just such questions.

At first glance, as discussed in the previous chapter, McCarthy would seem to have been virtually a prototype of the active-negative, and thus of the political man. There can be little doubt that, in broad outline, McCarthy was certainly the type who "strikes outward, energetically fighting against the forces that threaten him."[16]

Yet despite the surface similarities, upon closer examination, several key differences emerged, so that McCarthy could not be comfortably fitted into the active-negative category. As noted in Chapter 3, McCarthy was not a power seeker; he enjoyed his political career (at least up to his censure in 1954); he displayed little personalized anger against opponents; he manifested little or no genuine commitment to his cause; and, finally, once censured, he gave up the struggle virtually without a fight. In all these respects, McCarthy presented a picture quite unlike that of the typical active-negative. If, as Barber summarized it, the active-negative was one for whom "life is a hard struggle to achieve and hold power, hampered by the condemnations of a perfectionistic conscience,"[17] then McCarthy was certainly not an active-negative type.

The purpose of this chapter is to argue that these differences, which prevent McCarthy's being classified as a true active-negative (at the same time that he does not fall into any of the three other classifications), are linked to the absence of Lasswell's *r* in McCarthy's psychic economy. McCarthy's lack of any need to justify his more questionable actions—to rationalize his displacement of private motives onto the public arena— thus distinguishes him not only from Barber's active-negative, but also from Lasswell's political man, and from the Georges' "compulsive personality."[18] But if McCarthy's behavior cannot be understood in terms of those frameworks, how then can it be understood? Perhaps one should look more closely at Joseph McCarthy himself.

### The Absence of Rationalization

Richard Rovere, who knew McCarthy quite well after years of covering him in Washington, concluded in his 1959 biography that "the world took McCarthy seriously . . . , but he never really took himself seriously."[19] More recently, Edwin Bayley's study of McCarthy and the press cites reporter after reporter recalling: "It was just a big lark to Joe"; or "It was a sort of game for us, as it was for Joe"; or that McCarthy would urge journalists, "Tell me what you want and I'll say it."[20] In the words of Murrey Marder of the *Washington Post:*

He didn't give a damn about Communism or anything else. It was all a game with Joe. He'd browbeat a witness and then he'd go up and grin at him and expect him to be friendly.[21]

James Wechsler, editor of the *New York Post* in the 1950s, wrote after having been called before McCarthy's committee:

> McCarthy is a poker player, not a zealot. . . . I think he is one of the least passionate demagogues I have ever encountered. I am certain that he would have been happy to shake my hand and forget the whole thing if I had merely indicated that I had misjudged him and was prepared henceforth to write kinder things about him.[22]

Indeed, for Rovere, although McCarthy had great talents as a demagogue, "he lacked the most necessary and awesome of demagogic gifts—a belief in the sacredness of his own mission."[23]

It was clear to many that McCarthy's concern was minimally, if at all, for the crusade he had launched, but rather for the noise and excitement he might generate. Senator Charles Potter of Michigan once remarked to President Eisenhower, "It has become a nasty little game, and if you go back through the memory, you find that Joe gets bored with it very quickly if one particular act of vandalism is not scoring with the headlines."[24] Indeed, McCarthy's record was replete with instances of cases focused upon momentarily, only to be dropped when they failed to generate sufficient publicity. Quoting Rovere again:

> I know of nothing to suggest that he ever for a moment really thought the government was riddled with Communists; had he believed this, had he really cared, he would not have abandoned investigations merely from ennui or because of their failure to produce the headlines he expected. He was a political speculator, a prospector who drilled Communism and saw it come up a gusher. He liked his gusher but he would have liked any other just as well.[25]

Evidence for this lack of any deep emotional commitment to his political cause can also be found by examining McCarthy's private life—his offstage moments—for in his personal relations he was frequently a much different man. In private, far from being a thundering, brawling political infighter, Joe McCarthy was normally a gregarious, backslapping, jovial hail-fellow-well-met. Many of the reporters who considered him a complete fraud and a charlatan nonetheless found that they could not help but like him, and a fair number of people evidently maintained cordial relations with McCarthy despite their view of him as a rogue and a con man. Leonard Boudin, a left-wing attorney who represented a number of clients before McCarthy's committee acknowledged,

> I rather liked the man. He wasn't sanctimonious like most people in power on the right or left, and he didn't disguise what he was. He knew his investigations were a game, a grab for publicity.[26]

Senate colleagues were frequently mystified by McCarthy's behavior. As noted in Chapter 3, McCarthy would sometimes seek to disarm his Senate colleagues by mocking his own performance. He tried to treat matters as simply a political game. But some of McCarthy's Senate colleagues found it impossible to accept McCarthy's brand of game playing. Senator Herbert Lehman, a Democrat from New York, recalled:

> He was the most insensitive man I ever knew. You couldn't insult him. I would assail him in the most scathing terms, and after the debate he would come up grinning, throw his arm around my shoulder, and inquire, "How are you, Herb?" He seemed to have no sense of the fact that principles of right and wrong were involved. If anyone got hurt, it was too bad, but it was part of the game.[27]

One anonymous senator wondered at McCarthy's ability to separate his public and private worlds so easily: "He can be the most affable man in the world, and suddenly he will run the knife into you—particularly if the public is going to see it—and he will do it for no particular reason."[28]

One can find several cases, for example, in which McCarthy seemed genuinely surprised when those whom he had viciously attacked seemed unwilling shortly thereafter to accept his friendly greetings and playfulness.[29] Perhaps the single most startling case is that of a man whom McCarthy had mercilessly excoriated in a public hearing. Learning some time later that the man was now suffering deep financial problems,

> McCarthy sought the man out and said that he might be able to give him a hand with his financial problems. The man of course refused—no doubt thinking that McCarthy sought to rob him of his pride as well as his good name. In fact, McCarthy wanted neither; he wanted only the tumult occasioned by the session on the witness stand, and that he already had.[30]

The reality was that McCarthy simply could not comprehend the revulsion so many felt toward him and his activities. To him enemies were merely convenient targets of opportunity, not the subject of lifeling vendettas. McCarthy "could accuse a man of shielding Communists in the morning and in the afternoon meet and greet him on the floor, give him a wink and a manly hug."[31] For Paul Ringler of the *Milwaukee Journal,* McCarthy "was so totally amoral that he believed we should understand that this was all political gamesmanship—that no matter what he said, it shouldn't make any difference between friends."[32]

James Wechsler was surprised to sense no real animosity or rancor toward him on the part of a senator who was accusing him of secret sympathy for Communism:

I had the feeling that he really wanted me to understand his point of view. He seemed to be saying, "Look, bud, you've got your racket, and I've got mine, and this is it. There's no need to be such a wet blanket."[33]

Astonished that McCarthy would offer him a staff position after all the critical things he had written about the senator, Edwin Bayley of the *Milwaukee Journal* was told by McCarthy "Oh, that doesn't matter. If you worked for me you'd write it different."[34]

One major scholar of McCarthyism has concluded:

It was this disassociation of public and private roles which allowed McCarthy to distort, misrepresent, even lie, and yet through it all to retain what Richard Rovere has called his essential innocence. The lies, the violent accusations, the disregard for law and custom, all took place on the periphery of his personality. They never touched "Joe," the genial and charming Irishman who wanted nothing more than to love and be loved. They were all attributes of "McCarthy," the public figure he had conjured up from some bizarre notion of himself.[35]

Marder of the *Washington Post* noted that "when McCarthy made a charge against someone, his voice would rise to a high-pitched tremolo; then as he finished, he'd go back to his speaking voice, in a much lower register. It was as if he were two different persons."[36]

Thus, it seems clear that to those who saw McCarthy close up during the key years, there appeared to be a strong division between his public and private selves. It is therefore somewhat startling to find one of McCarthy's most recent biographers standing virtually alone in the assertion that "at some point in his post-Wheeling struggles Joe became persuaded of the overall truth of the Communist conspiracy charges that dominated his political career for the rest of his life."[37] Based upon interviews with McCarthy's widow, some friends and staffers, and Jack Anderson's recollection of a conversation with McCarthy, Reeves concludes that by early 1950, McCarthy had become "a zealot." At least one reviewer has ascribed to Reeves "a remarkable degree of credulity in accepting at face value many of the recollections of McCarthy's family and friends,"[38] but perhaps it is nonetheless possible to reconcile Reeves's view with the testimony cited above.

Three possibilities suggest themselves: (1) McCarthy said different things to different people; (2) McCarthy's views changed over time; or (3) McCarthy was sincerely anti-Communist at an abstract level, but was rather casual in terms of the specifics of his own crusade.

(1) It is possible that McCarthy, in speaking to reporters, was concerned primarily with winning their respect and friendship. Given that reporters are notoriously a cynical and hard-bitten crew, McCarthy could

have sensed that they might develop a sneaking fondness for a politician who did not appear to take himself too seriously. A show of cynicism might have been, for McCarthy, a way to become "one of the boys." Indeed, such an approach might have worked quite well, as attested to by the number of reporters who admitted that while they were repulsed by his tactics, they found themselves rather liking the private McCarthy. At a certain level, perhaps they could enjoy the rascality of a United States senator who could charge that 205 Communists were working in the State Department, and then announce to them, "Look, you guys. That was just a political speech to a bunch of Republicans. Don't take it seriously."[39]

At the same time, McCarthy's family, friends, and staffers might have seen a very different McCarthy. Surrounded by people who took him seriously and who took anti-Communism seriously, McCarthy might very well not have wanted to let them know that for him it was all a charade. In this respect, one cannot help but think of Roy Cohn's story of how McCarthy came to the issue of anti-Communism.

Cohn asserts that in late 1949, an army intelligence officer and two of his friends brought McCarthy a package of information concerning subversives in government.[40] Although reputable scholars have agreed that this is a most unlikely story,[41] it is certainly not impossible that McCarthy recounted this tale to Cohn because, at some point, Cohn seemed the right person to be told such a story.

This interpretation, of course, leaves open the question of whether McCarthy's cynicism and insincerity were genuine or not. Was the real McCarthy sincere about his anti-Communist crusade, but anxious not to appear too serious to the newspaper reporters he wanted to cultivate? Or was the real McCarthy the one the reporters saw, while friends and family and staffers were presented with a facade of sincerity? Clearly this can only be judged, if at all, in the context of an overall evaluation of the evidence.

(2) Perhaps, one might argue, McCarthy's views changed over time, so that although he began as a game player, he ended up as a true believer. John Steele of the United Press, for example, believed that "it was all fun and games for a while, but then he began taking it seriously. He became paranoiac."[42] Murrey Marder acknowledges that

it's probably true that a point came where he started to believe his own stuff, but I don't know if he was serious about communism in 1953 or just worried about people closing in on him.[43]

Even Richard Rovere, the strongest proponent of the view that McCarthy was first and foremost an opportunist, was willing to consider the possibility:

It is conceivable that in his later days he began to believe what he was saying and to imagine himself truly persecuted by his enemies; at times, during the Army-McCarthy hearings, he would fly into fits of what appeared genuine hysteria. He may by then have cast his spell over himself.[44]

"But even this is doubtful," Rovere ultimately concluded. In any event, Reeves's argument is that McCarthy was converted to sincere anti-Communism relatively early—shortly after the 1950 Wheeling speech, and therefore long before the 1954 Army-McCarthy hearings.[45] Reeves's assertion thus keeps him clearly at odds with the testimony of a great many people who watched McCarthy quite closely during his most important years.

(3) A final possibility that might allow some reconciliation of the conflicting views cited above would suggest that a distinction has to be made between anti-Communism as a general principle and the specific charges made by McCarthy.[46] Certainly there is nothing unreasonable in believing that McCarthy, like most Americans of his time was strongly anti-Communist and believed that there was a systematic Soviet effort to infiltrate American government.

It does not logically follow, however, that McCarthy actually believed that he could do much about this problem. Earl Latham has distinguished between the Communist *problem* and the Communist *issue*,[47] and perhaps it is fair to say that McCarthy was content to leave the problem to competent others while he took for himself the issue and the political profits that flowed from it. It is not hard, for example, to imagine that McCarthy had great confidence in the ability of such agencies as the FBI to deal with the problem at a real level, while he devoted himself to deriving some benefit for himself from the issue.

Thus, without any great thought being given to the matter, McCarthy made charges against people if they could be seen as having even the remotest of connections to the problem. He had his lists and his documents, and they were, after all, related to *something* having to do with security risks (whatever that might mean). Perhaps the people named were not so closely related to Communist subversion as the more judicious might have liked, but the general idea was enough. Politics was a rough and dirty game, and the goal was to win. Sometimes those in the game had to be ready to take a few punches that were not quite fair, but in the end, who would really suffer other than actual Communists—if he found any?

Indeed, as noted in the previous chapter, as early as the 1946 Senate race, McCarthy, meaning "no particular harm," had impugned the loyalty of his Democratic opponent, and then been warm and friendly to him offstage. In this context, one has no difficulty understanding how McCarthy, a year or so before he died, could meet a goverment official whose career he had ruined and ask him, "How come we never see you? What the hell are you trying to do—*avoid* us?"[48]

Therefore, although it may well have been the case that privately McCarthy was genuinely worried about the spread of Communism, it is very difficult to find much evidence of this concern in his day-to-day activities. As early as 1954, Rorty and Decter acknowledged that "whether McCarthy is 'sincere' is difficult for an outsider to determine. . . . The judgment as to Senator McCarthy's sincerity must be based on an examination of his record."[49] Thus, a close study of a series of McCarthy charges and how they were handled by the senator convinced the authors that on too many occasions McCarthy was content to raise serious charges that he never bothered to pursue.

> How are we to account for Senator McCarthy's failure to pinpoint or expose any element of infiltration or subversion? We must conclude either that he never seriously entertained these charges, or that he was not really interested in following them up, once they had been aired.[50]

As Richard Rovere put it,

> He would speak of Communists "with a razor poised over the jugular vein of this nation" in defense plants, in the Army, in radar laboratories. But he would stop talking and stop investigating the moment the headlines began to diminish in size and number, thus leaving our jugular in as much danger as before.[51]

McCarthy once announced that "the worst situation" was in the Central Intelligence Agency, but sensing that an investigation might be more trouble than it was worth, he was content to back off with a simple "I guess I'll skip it."[52]

In sum, the evidence (Reeves to the contrary notwithstanding) does seem to suggest that McCarthy was "a freeswinging soldier of fortune who . . . hit upon a good thing, anti-Communism."[53] The question that this raises then is, How does one go about seeking to understand and explain this crusader without commitment? How does one make sense of a political man who had no need to rationalize, of an active-negative who never felt guilty about his tactics?

Some possible answers to these questions are offered by analyzing the nature of Joseph McCarthy's political belief system, and two possible approaches suggest themselves. On the one hand, one might move toward a *causal* explanation for McCarthy's behavior, seeking to extract from the details of McCarthy's childhood and adolescence the factors that could have produced a political belief system like McCarthy's.[54]

On the other hand, one might try to move in the direction of a *coherent whole explanation,* in which one "advances a construct or set of constructs which help to make sense of the subject's behavior."[55] In this chapter, I will employ this second approach as a way of developing some ideas about the nature and functioning of McCarthy's political belief system. Then, in Chapter 5, I will turn my attention to the causal question—how McCarthy's political belief system came to develop in the manner it did.

## The Mind of Joseph McCarthy

I have concluded so far that the main factor distinguishing McCarthy from the various psychological types proposed by such political scientists as Lasswell, the Georges, and Barber is the absence in McCarthy of a need to rationalize his political behavior. Another way of saying the same thing is to point out that McCarthy was exceptionally unideological in his political orientation. McCarthy lacked a coherent, well-defined set of political ideas that would have allowed him to justify in terms of the public interest what he was doing.

Some opponents of McCarthy sought to paint him as another Hitler, but perceptive students of McCarthyism were quick to note some key differences:

> The totalitarian demagogue operates with something positive, with some idea or cause, which he himself believes in, yet perverts and exploits for his purposes. . . . The power with which he operates is fundamentally the power of the positive idea he stands for.
>
> Joe McCarthy is obviously something very different. He operates with no positive ideas; he stands *for* no cause, no program. . . . McCarthyism is thus the very apotheosis of negativity: it is a conglomeration of oppositions and resentments clinging around a vacuum.[56]

From the very beginnings of McCarthy's political career, one is hard put to find any evidence of strong political beliefs. Like his parents, McCarthy was a Democrat in the 1930s, "but his interest in and commitment to political thought ran no deeper than the prejudices of Tim and Bid."[57] He had no qualms about writing Republican editorials for a Republican newspaper in order to make some money, though he soon came to head the local Young Democrats, and in 1936 ran as the Democratic nominee for district attorney of Shawano County.

In 1938, McCarthy was elected a circuit judge in a nonpartisan election, and when he remerged into partisan politics in 1944, it was as a Republican candidate for a Senate nomination. Not surprisingly, Republican party activists were highly suspicious of what seemed to them an opportunistic move. When McCarthy again ran for a Republican Senate nomination in 1946, "he didn't offer substantive opinions on any subject to those whose support he requested."[58]

In the Senate, McCarthy's record did not place him clearly in any ideological camp. Indeed, when he launched his attack on domestic subversives in 1950, many ultraconservatives were surprised, for McCarthy "had hitherto been thought of—if at all—as a sort of moderate liberal, and many were delighted by his apparently sudden transformation."[59] As recently as 1948, for example, McCarthy had supported the liberal Harold Stassen for president against a movement for General Douglas MacArthur. Moreover, he had generally followed the internationalist Vandenberg line rather than the isolationism of the most conservative senators. While McCarthy did follow Taft on most domestic issues, this seemed to most observers a matter of supporting the Republican majority leader rather than a genuine commitment to conservative ideology. As late as 1956, a leading conservative working on McCarthy's staff "was hurt by the discovery that McCarthy wasn't a conservative at all. He could not be brought to repudiate the welfare state and was becoming, in fact, more and more like a left liberal in domestic affairs—favoring more public housing, more social security, more federal subsidies of all sorts."[60]

But if McCarthy was not a true conservative, perhaps he was—as the pluralists of the 1950s argued—fundamentally a populist. Perhaps it is in McCarthy's antiestablishment rhetoric, his attacks on striped-pants diplomats and Ivy League colleges, that one should seek the outlines of a coherent political belief system—an ideology. In their essays in *The New American Right*,[61] published in 1955, the pluralists—men like Daniel Bell, Richard Hofstadter, Peter Viereck, Talcott Parsons, and Seymour Martin Lipset—tried to make explicit what they saw as an underlying continuity between the Populists and Senator McCarthy. McCarthy's attacks on the eastern establishment and his support for the farmers made at least plausible the conception of McCarthy as one more heir to the dangerous populist tradition.

But as Michael Rogin has persuasively argued, McCarthy was not really part of this populist tradition at all. In *The Intellectuals and McCarthy,* Rogin argued that despite some superficial stylistic similarities, McCarthyism—both in its content and in its basis of support in the population—could better be understood in terms of a continuity with traditional midwestern conservatism. Hostility to the eastern establishment was not, after all, unique to the Populists, but was rather a pervasive attitude among midwesterners in general. Thus, Rogin concluded:

Godless radicals, intellectuals, and bureaucrats were targets of American conservatism many decades before McCarthyism. If he was more

extreme than many conservatives, he was extreme within that tradition.[62]

Ultimately, however, Rogin recognized that this ideological debate had
less to do with McCarthy himself than with the ideas and attitudes that
motivated his supporters. For although McCarthy could be seen as coming
out of an old American right, it was more accurate to characterize him as
one who employed its ideology, rather than as an ideologue himself. For
Rogin, "McCarthy himself was personally very different from other midwestern conservatives. Far from being a man of dangerous principles,
McCarthy was a thorough-going nihilist. . . . He believed in nothing."[63]

If it is true, however, that McCarthy was lacking in ideology to an
unusual degree for a political leader, how does this fact enable one to make
better sense of his political behavior? One can try to trace some of the
implications that flow from such a conclusion.

Philip Converse has suggested that ideology should be defined as a
belief system characterized by high constraint, great range, and a centrality of political ideas.[64] The key notion here is *constraint*.

> Constraint refers to the underlying structure of a belief system. If beliefs
> about specific political matters rest on some fundamental beliefs or
> values, then opinions about specific objects in the political world will
> take on a pattern. The result for the individual is that the world will
> seem more coherent and connected. The result for an observer or
> analyst of the individual's opinions is that opinions will be more predic-
> table and underlying political reasoning will be easier to interpret.[65]

Thus, ideology defined in this way is to be seen in terms of clusters of
political ideas held together in a way that makes rough sense and thereby
helps an individual to interpret the political world around him and to
develop attitudes toward the new political stimuli constantly bombarding
him. With the aid of an ideology, a person is able to feel that his thoughts
and actions are appropriate and comprehensible, not merely random, ad
hoc responses of the moment. Possession of an ideology enables a person
to view his actions as mature, logically connected, and appropriate in
terms of some broader societal perspective.

In general, it seems logical to conclude that "the closer one moves to
the stage of politics . . . the more one is likely to encounter actors with
highly formed political orientations, not only on a matter of political
preference but also vis-à-vis the nature and operating principles of the
political process itself."[66] Political actors are likely to have relatively well
defined ideologies, and these are likely to play a major role in the processes of rationalization that enable them to function satisfactorily in the
political arena.

The hypothesis presented here is that such an ideological mode of thought was not attained by Joseph McCarthy, and that there was, therefore, only the most minimal constraint at work in his political belief system. What McCarthy did in the world of politics required no elaborate justification in terms of any preexisting pattern of thought linking his actions to broader social goals. McCarthy's needs, by themselves, justified his actions, so far as he was concerned.

The consequences of such an unconstrained, unstructured cognitive style can be seen most clearly in children at what has been called the "pre-ideological level":

> We may note the arguments that leap so suddenly from topic to topic . . . the seizing on odd and apparently irrelevant details, and the apparently random juxtapositions of details; the repeated bending of reality to the demands of a momentary stream of thought.[67]

One cannot help but be struck by the resemblance of this description to the depictions, by those who watched him closely, of McCarthy at work. To Rovere, "his tongue was always loose and wagging; he would say anything that came into his head and worry later, if at all, about defending what he had said."[68] Washington correspondents complained that McCarthy "was difficult to cover because he talked in fragments and non sequiturs"; that "the man just talked circles. . . . Most of it didn't make sense"; and that dealing with him "was like trying to pin down a blob of mercury."[69] "Talking to Joe was like putting your hands in a bowl of mush," recalled George Reedy, who worked for the United Press in that era.[70]

Other observers have noted McCarthy's unusual notions about what constituted evidence. "Documents, documents, documents—he was always loaded with them. The bulging briefcase—the scholar's toolbox—became to him what snapping red galluses and a stream of tobacco juice were to the older Southern demagogues."[71] Yet despite what seemed a real fact fetishism, McCarthy handled what he called evidence in the most casual, offhand manner. Old congressional subcommittee lists of "incidents of inefficiencies" were transformed into lists of "card-carrying Communists."[72] Called on to defend his charges that there were Communists in the State Department, McCarthy described "cases" of two people who had been *applicants* for State Department jobs two years earlier, a person who had once been in the Commerce Department, a person "not important insofar as Communistic activities are concerned," a person for whom "there is nothing in the files to disprove his Communist connections," and one person notable "in that it is the direct opposite of the cases I have been reading. . . . I do not confuse this man as being a Communist." Nor had he ever worked for the State Department.[73]

As early as McCarthy's involvement in the investigation of the Malmédy massacre, Rovere had found himself offered piles and piles of documents to read. These documents, McCarthy had insisted, when put together would make immediately clear "the true story" of what had happened at Malmédy. Innocent to McCarthy's ways in 1949, Rovere became involved in a surreal scene where meaningless document after meaningless document was placed before him with the assurance that very soon these "pieces of the jigsaw puzzle" would make sense to him. Of course they never did, and after a while Rovere politely excused himself to go on to other things.[74]

Republican senator Margaret Chase Smith encountered a similar problem when she requested to see the "photostatic copies" that McCarthy claimed proved the truth of his Wheeling allegations. Unable to understand the relevance of the documents to McCarthy's charges, Smith began to doubt her own abilities. "But the more I listened to Joe and the more I read the papers he held in his hand, the less I could understand what he was up to. And more and more I began to wonder whether I was as stupid as I had thought."[75]

Senator Lehman at one point took McCarthy up on his offer to show to any senator an Owen Lattimore letter from which he was reading on the Senate floor.

> To what must have been his astonishment, Senator Lehman accepted the offer and walked across the floor toward McCarthy's desk. "I yield no further," McCarthy said. And with excellent reason, for in truth he had not been quoting in context or out of context; he simply had *not been quoting at all.* He had simply invented, standing there on the Senate floor, lines that served his purpose at the moment and attributed them to Owen Lattimore. This became known only a bit later when the letter turned up as part of a printed transcript.[76]

Thus, even Thomas Reeves, one of McCarthy's more sympathetic biographers, concludes that the senator's approach to his anti-Communist crusade was unusually haphazard and scattershot. Reeves makes a most useful comparison with another Communist hunter of the period:

> Richard Nixon, for example, studied issues, institutions, and personalities; his manipulations were based upon a shrewd understanding of how things worked and what it took to achieve carefully planned goals. McCarthy, on the other hand, had no goals (beyond his re-election), and thought nothing out in advance. As had long been his style, he shot from the hip, bluffed, lied.[77]

From such descriptions, a great deal of McCarthy's political style clearly emerges—a style that could not help but drive his opponents to the heights of frustration. It is not a style one would normally expect to encounter in the United States Senate. And once encountering it, how could one hope to respond to it? Given certain basic expectations regarding rules of logic and rationality, would it not prove extremely difficult, perhaps impossible, to combat someone apparently not bound by such rules? One cannot help but sympathize with Senator Brien McMahon, a Democrat from Connecticut, who, in the aftermath of Wheeling,

> made thirty-four vain attempts to have McCarthy submit to a testing of his claims against reason and evidence—to conduct the debate within the framework of rationality as rationality is codified in the Senate rules. He would not explain, he would not amplify, he would not qualify—yet, and this was always part of his method, he would employ all the cant of rational discourse, all its paraphernalia, all its moods and tones and tenses.[78]

It is not difficult to envision Majority Leader Scott Lucas, a Democrat from Illinois, listening to this debate, "the absurdity of it all" so clear to him, "completely confident that no one could take McCarthy seriously."[79]

Although McCarthy's prepared speeches adhered more closely to a framework of rationality, it seems evident that this was an externally imposed rationality, representing the world view of those who wrote the speeches. Rovere comments on how out of character in many ways was McCarthy's famous 1951 speech attacking General George Marshall. A rather scholarly critique of Allied High Command strategy during World War II, the speech was enlivened by additions McCarthy and his staff aides made, accusing Marshall of taking part in "infamy so black as to dwarf any previous such venture in the history of man." A few days later, McCarthy added the charge that Marshall "would sell his grandmother for any advantage."[80] The rather scholarly journalist who had prepared the original material moaned to himself about the uses to which his manuscript had been put, but never complained publicly.[81]

The complaints about McCarthy's haphazard style were frequent, even among those generally supportive of his crusade. Robert Taft complained in 1951: "I thought if he was going into this fight he ought to be carefully prepared and get some experts to help him. He agreed in principle but never did much about it."[82] When McCarthy finally got his so-called experts in 1953—Roy Cohn and G. David Schine—they did have an initial influence in shaping McCarthy's direction. "They had a sizable staff below them and McCarthy above them, but the strategies were theirs."[83] But though Cohn and Schine managed to give some shape to McCarthy's performance in 1953 and 1954, they were not very successful in keeping his attention focused very long either. And when Schine was drafted, Cohn's reaction played a key role in bringing about McCarthy's downfall in the Army-McCarthy hearings.

One can only sum up by concluding that, in the long run, the anarchic pattern of McCarthy's accusations, his failure to follow up on his charges, his casual attitude toward what he claimed was evidence all make clear that the senator was operating, not according to some master plan or coherent strategy of attack, but rather on a more purely intuitive basis. The key criterion in his crusade was what worked, and this was defined largely in terms of public attention and notoriety.

### The Absence of Ideological Thought

What can be concluded from the evidence suggesting that McCarthy was the possessor of an unusually rambling and disorganized political belief system? One useful perspective emerges from the work of Giovanni Sartori on the nature of ideological thought.[84] For Sartori, ideology is not to be viewed as a component of the belief system, but rather as one of its possible states. Drawing upon the work of Milton Rokeach regarding "open" and "closed" minds, Sartori hypothesizes an ideological mentality characterized by a closed cognitive structure—defined as "a state of dogmatic impermeability both to evidence and argument," and a pragmatic mentality, identified with an open cognitive structure—defined as "a state of mental permeability."[85]

However, cognitive status—openness or closedness—is but one dimension of the political belief system. "Emotive status," or "affect" is the second dimension, and this defines the *intensity* with which elements of the belief system are held. Combining these two dimensions enables Sartori to produce a fourfold typology of political belief systems.

The typology can be explained as follows:

> Definition: Whenever ideology and pragmatism are confronted dichotomously, and thereby conceptualized as polar types, *ideology* is a belief system based on i) fixed elements, characterized by ii) strong affect and iii) closed cognitive structure. *Pragmatism* is, conversely, a belief system based on i) flexible elements characterized by ii) weak affect and iii) open cognitive structure.[86]

Ideology and pragmatism are, of course, ideal types, unlikely to be found so neatly and clearly defined in the belief systems of real people, but it certainly seems clear that McCarthy's lack of ideology places him squarely in Sartori's pragmatic category. Sartori does assert that those in this category lack "outward dynamism" in the sense of not being motivated toward outward expansion, "either in the form of proselytism or of overt aggression."[87] However, although this seems rather different from McCarthy's case, it is possible to suggest that Sartori is placing excessive emphasis on ideas as a source of political activism, and failing to give sufficient weight to nonrational factors. Certainly there are sources of political energy other than the desire to advance one's ideas—one has merely to think of the striving for power or glory that have only peripheral connection to specific political ideas.

The suggestion made here, then, is that Joseph McCarthy's political beliefs were weakly held ones with relatively little emotional investment made in them. McCarthy flitted from issue to issue as opportunity beckoned, but no real moral passion was ever invested in his espousal of one view or another. Even his crusade against Communism at home—his great moment on the public stage—was marked, as noted earlier, by an astonishing lack of zeal. From all the evidence, McCarthy appears to have stumbled upon domestic subversion as an issue almost by accident, played upon it in an extremely erratic and haphazard manner, and never truly merged his identity with it in the way that, for example, a Woodrow Wilson came to identify with the Versailles Treaty.

For James Wechsler, McCarthy was "the least passionate demagogue" he had ever met. Certainly all the game playing described above supports the conclusion that McCarthy did not take very seriously what he was doing. At the same time, despite having what has been described as a "good mind and highly retentive, almost photographic, memory,"[88] McCarthy had for years displayed an exceptional sloppiness of thought.

TABLE 3

IDEOLOGY AND PRAGMATISM AS POLAR OPPOSITES

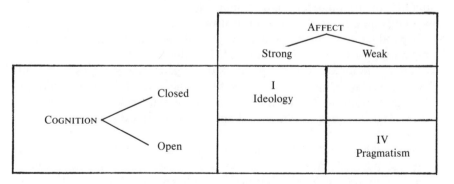

SOURCE: Sartori, "Politics, Ideology, and Belief Systems," p. 405.

For Reeves, McCarthy in 1950 "had long since revealed his capacity for uncritical belief and an ability to ignore the promptings of his intellect."[89] As an attorney in Wisconsin, "McCarthy had never developed a deep understanding of the law. Often he was unprepared for a jury case and tried to compensate with style."[90] As a judge, in one extremely important case, McCarthy "subjected all the participants to a rambling discourse about his thoughts on the . . . case," and as if that were not enough, "in a flight into fantasy . . . expounded at length beyond any technical rules of law."[91] In the end, "most of McCarthy's decision was based on no evidence whatsoever; it sprang from his vivid imagination."[92]

It seems a fair conclusion that McCarthy thus possessed no set of anchoring beliefs about the pursuit of the public interest that might have helped him to measure his actions in terms of some overall strategic conception. No underlying philosophy or rationale existed that might have given point to the things he said and did in the course of his campaign against domestic subversion. Certain consequences flowed from this.

It is no secret that Americans have generally had something of an intellectual prejudice against ideology and the implication that reality should be forced into some preexisting structure of thought. Yet if there is validity to this view, there is also validity to the view that pragmatism yields its own, if somewhat different problems. If ideology carried to an extreme cuts one off from the real world, then pragmatism carried to a comparable extreme perhaps puts one too much in contact with that world.

It seems evident that a totally pragmatic belief system could not actually function in the political world. Some organizing ideas must exist in order for a person to be able to screen, channel, and interpret the political world. It is impossible for anyone to analyze, in a vacuum, every new stimulus in the political environment, independent of any vision of the meaning and purposes of the political world.

Depending upon one's personality and culture, one may be more or less pragmatic, more or less ideological, but this can be true only within certain broad limits. At some point of ideologism, one becomes so cut off from empirical reality, so dominated by the need to fit all facts into one's ideological framework, that functioning in the real world is severely hampered. Theory ceases to be tested against facts, and disaster is likely to ensue.

On the other hand, one may move so far toward the pragmatic mentality that one becomes in essence a free-floating participant in the political world, anchored by no set of ideas that would enable others to make sense of one's actions. Whatever current happened to be at work in the political world at any given moment could carry such a person along no matter where he might be led. Basic needs would continue to require satisfaction of course, but the internal pressure of such needs would interact with the outside world's forces in such a way as to produce a pattern of activity without logical coherence or predictability. The absence of constraint would be complete.

In the case of Joseph McCarthy, I suggest that his lack of ideological underpinnings left him with an extremely pragmatic political belief system (perhaps *hyperpragmatic* would not be too strong a term), so that for him, political ideas were "open to argument and/or evidence *and furthermore, to convenience.*"[93] For McCarthy, political ideas were purely instrumental, weapons to be held onto for precisely as long as they proved useful to the attainment of his private purposes.

Some might well regard the situation described above as simply the definition of a politician, but McCarthy is useful precisely because he shows how far from this archetype most politicians really are, and why this seemingly quintessential political mode of thought has its built-in limitations. If it is true that to believe absolutely in a cause can lead a politician to disaster, as happened with Woodrow Wilson and the Versailles Treaty, it would appear to be just as true that to believe in nothing is no guarantee of success either.

Political man, the compulsive personality, and the active-negative type also make use of political ideas to help them satisfy their private motives, but the fact that these ideas are, at some level, genuinely believed in seems to make a considerable difference. Such ideas may well have to accommodate themselves to the twists and turns of the underlying needs of such political leaders, but the ideas themselves nevertheless continue to exercise at least some restraining power upon their actions. Because they are believed, it becomes necessary to build up a logical structure around them, and this structure creates constraints upon action.

Normally, political science, when it has examined elite belief systems, has been able to find relatively well organized cognitive structures, and has been able to find fairly logical connections to actions and behavior.[94] But McCarthy's political belief system resembles much more what Converse called "mass belief systems"[95]—cognitive structures characterized by disorganization and lack of constraint. Thus, to the extent that McCarthy was a key actor in the era that bears his name, he might well be viewed as injecting the style of "mass" political thinking into what is far more legitimately seen as an elite conflict.

While the pluralists of the 1950s saw McCarthyism as an example of mass politics and its potential dangers, Michael Rogin's 1967 study successfully demonstrated that McCarthyism really had a relatively small base in the population at large. McCarthyism, then, could be much better understood as an elite phenomenon—a weapon employed by the Republican party to regain the presidency after twenty years of Democratic domination. While strongly supported by empirical evidence, however, this view could not account for the tone of the McCarthy era, a tone much more associated with previous mass uprisings such as Populism. The suggestion here is that McCarthy provides that missing link. It was McCarthy's political belief system that injected an unusually strong note of irrationality into what was essentially a typical struggle between the Democratic and Republican parties.

Joseph McCarthy's political ideas were never very well integrated or even connected, and the personal motivations lying behind his actions were therefore allowed to exercise unusually direct and unmediated control over his behavior. Without any real need to feel that some genuine public purpose tied his actions together into a coherent pattern, McCarthy remained free to respond to his political environment without much semblance of long-term rationality as he pursued his own ends.

There is, of course, at least some resemblance, when McCarthy is described in the terms employed above, to the Machiavellian personality outlined in the work of Christie and Geis.[96] The Machiavellian, like McCarthy, was seen as an "operator," more interested in manipulation than in substantive ends, not much concerned with conventional morality, and not very committed to any ideology.

Yet there remains at least one fundamental difference between McCarthy and the Machiavellian. The latter is a strategic thinker, always thinking ahead in terms of the best approach to "winning." Indeed, the "high Mach" is seen as almost "over-rational" in his dealings with others, able to display exceptionally strong self-control as he moves toward the goal he has set for himself. He is a good improviser, but his improvisations take place within the context of a strong strategic conception.

Of McCarthy, on the other hand, it was said that "he had intense ambition and drive, yet never planned ahead. While he was accused of long-range plans to make himself a national leader, he never knew at 9 P.M. what he would be doing at 9 A.M. the next day."[97] Laughing off a publisher's proposal that he write a book on McCarthy's "secret plan" to become president, Murrey Marder of the *Washington Post* explained that "Joe doesn't have a plan about who he's going to lunch with tomorrow. He never has any plans."[98] Roy Cohn certainly seems close to the mark when he reports that McCarthy "was a hard, tough fighter . . . he was not a devious man, not a plotter, not a shrewd calculator of the odds, not a manipulator."[99] As a boxer, McCarthy had been the wild slugger, succeeding largely by being willing to accept great pain while he inflicted greater pain. As a poker player, he won not by knowing the odds, but because "you get to a point where you don't care what McCarthy's got in the hole—all you know is that it's too costly to stay in the game."[100] Clearly, while there were some similarities, McCarthy was not Christie and Geis's Machiavellian.

Wherein does the difference lie? Both McCarthy and the high Mach are nonideological. What may distinguish them is the difference in the roots of their lack of ideology. Ideology has been seen as having its origins in both cognitive and moral development.[101] In order to think ideologically, it is necessary to attain fairly sophisticated cognitive and moral levels. Since both McCarthy and the high Mach appear to display relatively little concern for conventional morality as they pursue their ends, it seems logical to point to cognitive differences.

If the Machiavellian is a good planner, possesses a strong strategic sense, and is highly rational, then it seems fair to conclude that his cognitive structures are of a fairly high order. While his thinking is flexible, it is not disorganized and disconnected. There must be present a relatively strong sense of reality and of how the world works.

McCarthy, on the other hand, at least in relation to the political world, appears to have had an unusually fragmented and disjointed cognitive structure, one in which ideas were not terribly well integrated or connected. Thus, what is important in understanding the ultimate failure of McCarthy is the lack of control that allowed him to act in a manner that did not permit of much logical explanation or defense.

McCarthy could of course provide for public consumption an overall justification for his anti-Communist crusade, but he could never convincingly demonstrate that his means were logically connected to the ends he claimed to be pursuing. Even many of his supporters were forced into the position of decrying McCarthy's methods while insisting that he was right in the substance of his general charge.

Thus, while any single action of McCarthy could have been viewed as rational for the moment in which it took place, the long-range result of all his actions combined was the creation in the minds of political leaders, and even some portion of the public, of a sense of deep irrationality at work. While there was certainly a "psycho-logic"—the satisfaction of private motives—at work in McCarthy's behavior, a clearly articulated public logic that could explain so many strange and erratic actions in terms of McCarthy's stated goal was notably absent. McCarthy's actions were therefore left to speak for themselves, and this could not help but foster a growing perception of McCarthy as a man out of control. Republican party leaders were initially willing to overlook the absence of a logic in McCarthy's actions, so long as his target was the Democrats. Thus, McCarthy was legitimatized in the eyes of a substantial segment of the public. But when McCarthy's actions began to threaten Republican interests, in 1953 and 1954, that legitimatization came to be withdrawn and sanctions were brought to bear.

That McCarthy did not himself really believe in his cause might not have mattered had he at least been able to operate within the normal framework of rationality as defined in American politics. So long as the public believed him, perhaps his own views would not have been terribly important. Indeed, the portrait of the high Mach seems to suggest that the likelihood of his succeeding is enhanced by the absence of such "irrelevant affect" (in Christie and Geis's phrase) as moral or ideological beliefs.

It may be, however, that such success depends on not being too obvious about what one is doing. Others, at least, must believe in the "rationalization in the public interest" that one puts forward as justification for actions that might otherwise be suspect. In this respect, McCarthy's style can be seen as simply too blatant. Given a political belief system that imposed virtually no controls upon his actions, each action became too obviously a pure response to private needs. When half the Republican party decided to stop vouching for McCarthy and thereby withdrew from him the "rationality by proxy" he had in effect been granted, his time in the sun was at an end.

In sum, therefore, one may conclude that while a political leader can function (perhaps quite successfully) without any need to rationalize his actions to himself, those actions must nonetheless at least *be capable of being rationalized*. Actions that are purely the product of private motives, and that cannot be understood in any other way, are ultimately vulnerable to the decision of the political system to punish such actions. This was the lesson McCarthy would learn when the Senate censured him in 1954.

### The Impulsive Style in Politics

One of the most useful aspects of the work of James David Barber in the field of political personality has been his elaboration of the concept of *style*.[102] Style is a particularly valuable concept in that its definition—the means a person adopts in order to cope with his world—allows one to link personality variables to actual functioning in a political role. Unlike role theory, which is tied to a person's conception of a particular office or position, the concept of style permits one to draw conclusions as to how a subject will behave in a political office, based upon his or her general stance toward the world and the problems it presents.[103]

The final question I want to consider, therefore, is whether the style of behavior displayed by Senator McCarthy corresponds to any broader syndrome constituting a distinct and identifiable style so far not described in the literature of political science. Since it would appear that McCarthy does not fall into the general pattern of Lasswell's political man, the Georges' compulsive personality, Barber's active-negative type, or Christie and Geis's Machiavellian, one wonders where precisely McCarthy would be classified.

The hypothesis set forth here is that there exists in politics an "im-

pulsive style"—perhaps similar in some outward respects to the types
mentioned above, but ultimately quite different in important respects and
in terms of its internal dynamics. This style can best be understood in
terms of the empirical studies of Jerome Kagan and the clinical work of
David Shapiro. [105]

Kagan's work was aimed at understanding the poor schoolwork of some
children. His development, at Harvard in 1964, of the Matching Familiar
Figures Test (MFFT) allowed him to measure a dimension he termed
*Reflection-Impulsivity,* or conceptual tempo. In conditions of uncertainty,
an impulsive child was likely to answer quickly, with little reflection, and
process an incorrect hypothesis with little or no critical analysis of likely
accuracy.

> In these situations some children report the first classification that
> occurs to them or carry out the first solution sequence that appears
> appropriate. The reflective children, on the other hand, charac-
> teristically delay before reporting a classification or carrying out a
> solution hypothesis. [106]

Impulsive children were likely to give the first answer that occurred to
them, so that "their strategy of problem-solving has a shotgun character;
the child fires a fusillade of answers in the hope that one will be correct, or,
perhaps, because he needs immediate feedback from the environment to
inform him of the quality of his performance." [107] Moreover, Kagan found
that

> A tendency toward reflection versus impulsivity displayed a stability
> over time and a generality across tasks that is unusual for psychological
> attributes and tempts one to conclude that this dimension is a basic
> component of a child's behavioral organization. [108]

David Shapiro, from his clinical study, concluded that there was indeed
an "impulsive style."

> This group . . . has a general mode of action in common. . . . It also has
> in common other essential features associated with this mode of ac-
> tion—a style of cognition and, of particular interest, a characteristic and
> distinctive type of subjective experience of action and motivation to
> action. [109]

The impulsive type, in Shapiro's view, was best characterized as moved to
act by whim, urge, or impulse. "Giving in" was the most common feeling
experienced by impulsives, betokening an impairment of the sense of
active intention and deliberateness. The impulsive type found himself

unable to choose a course of action and then stick to it. While all people experience impulse at one time or another, for the impulsive it was the regular and predominant style. Interestingly, the sense of not being responsible allowed the impulsive—in contrast to other neurotics—an apparent self-confidence and a general lack of anxiety.[110]

Shapiro isolated three formal characteristics of impulsive action: (1) speediness, in the sense that there was little time between thought and action; (2) abruptness and discontinuity from one action to another; and (3) unplannedness of actions.[111] Impulses became actions in a way that seemed to "short-circuit" certain active cognitive processes.

For most people, a whim or impulse normally triggers a complex process that puts that impulse into a context of long-range interests, values, and emotional connections and helps relate it to current aims and interests. In most cases, such impulses will either be repressed (if they are wildly removed from what makes sense in one's life), or alternatively, they will be reflected upon to the point that they mature into full-blown, deliberate choices that are actively made.

For the impulsive, however, there is "a deficiency in the integration of a whim or impulse with a pre-existing organization of stable and continuous aims and interests."[112] Impulsives tend to have remarkably few interests, values, or goals beyond the immediate concerns of their own lives. Lacking such integrative equipment, they are unable to resist impulses that develop within them. Without long-range goals, the frustrations and tensions engendered by the desire of the moment cannot be controlled, and immediate gratification becomes necessary.

It is impossible to read such a description and not think of Senator McCarthy in his day-to-day maneuvers, casually picking new "Communists" to attack, and always able to milk his choice for just enough publicity before switching to a new target. It is interesting to note that many of the metaphors developed by journalists and scholars to convey the sense of how McCarthy operated involve some aspect of impulsiveness: McCarthy as child or juvenile delinquent;[113] McCarthy as barroom brawler;[114] McCarthy as gambler and poker player;[115] McCarthy as poltergeist.[116] One biographer saw the Wisconsin senator as a buccaneer:

> McCarthy, with a privateer's bravado, would lay aboard an adversary of superior weight against all prudence and reason, and the very impetuousness and recklessness of his onslaught often enabled him to beat down opposition and make off with his prize. Because he often acts from different motives than the majority of mankind, the freebooter can cut through conventional courses, and attack or scurry away as the exigency of the moment may require.[117]

In the words of his own attorney, Edward Bennett Williams, "McCarthy was a man who could never resist the temptation to touch a sign which said WET PAINT."[118] "Impetuous," "unpredictable," "reckless," and "uncontrollable" are the phrases one finds over and over again used as descriptions of McCarthy's character. "He was impatient, overly aggressive, overly dramatic. He acted on impulse," Roy Cohn writes.[119] When it came to finances, McCarthy "made money to spend it, gamble with it, give it away . . . He rarely knew how much he was carrying, how much he owed, or how much he would need to get through the week."[120]

McCarthy seems very much the "unanchored personality," lacking stable and continuous aims, interests, and values. Lacking stable mental structures to anchor his behavior, the impulsive becomes subject to whatever whim happens to catch his fancy. Where the compulsive type's behavior seems to be governed by the motto "I must," the impulsive's actions seem to be a matter of "I can't help it."

Barber's active-negative type is a person living with a sense of compulsion,

> a man under orders, required to concentrate, to produce, to follow out his destiny as he sees it. At any given moment, he feels bound by what he has already undertaken, already promised, already committed. The central conflict between virtuousness and power-seeking is never resolved, but is massively denied in the feeling that whatever one does, one has no choice.[121]

The impulsive, by contrast, feels himself to be acting without any very clear sense of motivation or desire, yet also without any sense of morality or duty. He is moved almost entirely by his immediate needs and concerns and is therefore interested primarily in immediate gratification.

Such impulsiveness has both cognitive and moral roots. Piaget has commented that "having will is to possess a permanent scale of values. . . . And conversely, not having will, means knowing only unstable and momentary values, not being able to rely upon a permanent scale of values."[122] This suggests a moral stuntedness, the absence of a moral compass, so that a person's actions will tend to be limited mainly by the extent to which the environment is able to enforce such limits. The relevance of the moral dimension in understanding impulsiveness is certainly deserving of further study. Here, however, the focus is on the cognitive dimension, since it is this dimension that seems best to account for McCarthy's differences from the Machiavellian.

Shapiro speaks of a unique "impulsive style of cognition" in which attention is quickly and completely captured by the immediate, personally relevant aspects of a situation.[123] Virtually no thought is given to possible alternatives or to possibilities for long-range satisfactions. The impulsive lacks judgment and is reckless in the sense that he is likely to rush into situations without really analyzing them. For the impulsive, cognition does not stabilize against impulse, but rather "conspires" to aid it.

The impulsive type does not merely lack the data that would inform a rational choice; his cognitive style actually prevents him from searching out such information and organizing it. The impulsive, rather than considering options, does what "looks good" at the moment.

> When we say, therefore, that the impulsive person's judgment is poor, we say something about his cognition in general, namely that it is deficient in certain active processes. Where the normal person searches, weighs, and develops an initial impression, the impulsive person experiences a more immediate response; his initial impression, hunch, or guess becomes, without much further development, his final conclusion. his thinking is "off the top of his head."[124]

Thus, for the impulsive, the desire to act finds no restraining force in his cognitive structure, and to these individuals then, the world appears "discontinuous and inconstant—a series of opportunities, temptations, frustrations, sensuous experiences and fragmented impressions."[125] Planning, concentration, and logical objectivity are all impaired to the point that, in Piaget's terms, the impulsive is the prisoner of a passive and concrete cognitive style.[126] The impulsive's thought is passive in the sense that his attention is easily and completely captured by whatever aspect of a situation strikes him first, thus ending any further search or analysis. Yet he can be relatively easily distracted after a short while by whatever new, striking element captures his attention. In addition, the impulsive's thought is concrete to the extent that he tends to see things only in their most obvious, immediately personally relevant aspects. Potentialities and logical implications of a situation are unlikely to be considered.

In this context, one cannot help but think of Rovere's Joe McCarthy.

> Joe McCarthy was never, I think, a truly Machiavellian figure. He had no strategic sense—no cunning that would serve him tomorrow as well as today. He improvised from moment to moment, and some of his improvisations turned out badly.[127]

McCarthy's improvisations of the moment frequently brought him the headlines he craved, and usually there was no harm done. Asked to come up with a story for two bored reporters, he might reach into his pocket for a pen and begin writing out a subpoena for former President Truman. If the news media's attention flagged, he would announce an investigation of Communist infiltration of the CIA. Episodes of this sort usually amounted to nothing, of course. Indeed, so long as McCarthy had the tacit support of the Republican leadership, the translation of his impulses into action against the Democrats caused him few problems. But as the political tides turned after 1952 with the election of Dwight Eisenhower to the presidency, such impulsive actions as the attack on General Ralph Zwicker, which "just flashed out,"[128] came to seem more and more dangerous to the Republican party and were thus less and less tolerable to it.

Still, so long as the political environment was favorable, McCarthy was able to go a long way, and the explanation for this would appear to lie in the adaptive elements of the impulsive style. The impulsive's actions, given the sometimes zany quality they convey, make it easy to underestimate the extent to which such a style can be highly successful. Like the Machiavellian, but at a much more intuitive, rather than reasoned, level, the impulsive can operate in a surprisingly skillful manner.

Impulsives are frequently keenly intelligent, in the sense of an intelligence well suited to competent execution of their short-range aims. Although impulsive behavior may appear chaotic and random to the casual observer, it is rather the case that "those impulsive actions that are, from one standpoint, so erratic and unmindful of consequences are nevertheless typically executed with perfectly adequate and, in many cases, even superb competency."[129] Impulsives often possess an extraordinarily sure sense of other people's concerns and weaknesses and are able to manipulate these so as to attain their own immediate ends.

> It is well known, for example, that many impulsive people possess considerable social facility and are often socially very charming and engaging. They may also be quite playful, in contrast, for instance, to the heavy, overdeliberate, and somewhat dull quality of some obsessive-compulsive people, and given a good intellectual endowment, they may be witty and entertaining.[130]

Thus, particularly in an environment "where readiness for quick action or expression and/or a facility and competence of a sort that may be developed in pursuit of immediate and egocentric interest can be useful,"[131] the impulsive style may prove quite adaptive. It was McCarthy's good fortune, in the period from 1950 to 1954, to find a political environment where the willingness to speak and act without much thought on the matter of domestic Communists would bring great success.

Given Republican political elites willing to legitimatize what he said and did, and Democratic political elites who, in their earlier attempts to ward off charges of being soft on Communism may also have helped to legitimatize the issue of domestic subversion, McCarthy found an exceptionally hospitable atmosphere for what, in retrospect, strikes many as clearly absurd charges. In the short run, McCarthy could hardly have fared more spectacularly. But the impulsive, precisely because his perspective is such a short-range one, is unlikely to succeed for very long, and the case of McCarthy demonstrates this quite well. By 1954, the Army-McCarthy hearings had set the stage for the senator's political demise, and it was the Fred Fisher episode that came to symbolize the end of McCarthy's reign of terror—the moment in which the impulsive style carried him over the precipice.

During the course of the hearings, McCarthy grew increasingly perturbed at what he regarded as the harrying of his aide and confidant, Roy Cohn, by Army counsel Joseph Welch. With very little apparent thought or consideration of the matter, McCarthy went into his characteristic mode of response—attack.

A junior member of Welch's Boston law firm, Fred Fisher, had been deliberately kept out of the Army-McCarthy hearings by Welch because Fisher had at one time belonged to the National Lawyers Guild, named by the Justice Department as a Communist front organization. Both Roy Cohn and McCarthy's attorney, Edward Bennett Williams, had urged the senator not to bring up the matter in the hearings, and McCarthy had promised not to. Thus, when McCarthy launched the attack in the Senate hearing room, Cohn could be seen vigorously shaking his head, silently pleading with McCarthy not to pursue the matter any further. Acknowledging that "Mr. Cohn would rather not have me go into this," McCarthy nonetheless bore in, refusing to drop the matter, although its irrelevance was clear to all, and its only consequence, apart from a momentary diversion, could be the damage done to a young, rising attorney.

Joseph Welch, seemingly close to tears, responded with great emotion: "Have you no sense of decency, sir, at long last? Have you left no sense of decency?" The audience broke into tumultuous applause, and in the view of most observers, it was that moment which turned the tide irrevocably against McCarthy. The public watching at home on television did not like what it saw, and this emboldened the Senate to move against the Wisconsin senator.

Particularly interesting, however, was McCarthy's own reaction to what had happened in the hearing room.

> When, later, McCarthy at last found someone who would speak to him, he held out his hands, palms upward, and said, "What did I *do?*"[132]

Rovere goes on: "He knew what he had said, of course, but I genuinely believe that he did not know what he had *done.*"[133] McCarthy had simply done what had leaped to mind, and he could not quite understand what all the fuss was about.

For McCarthy, there had been nothing to stop the translation of thought into action—no mediating moral or cognitive structures to cause him to consider and reconsider the wisdom and propriety of his action. McCarthy had meant no real harm; he had merely been playing out the game in the only way he knew how. He had always done it this way, and now, suddenly, the rules seemed to have been changed in midgame.

Like the compulsive, whom the Georges view as potentially subject to self-defeating behaviors,[134] the impulsive, too, appears ultimately to reach the point where his actions assure his defeat. Indeed, in both cases, one might attribute such irrational behavior to the same source—the weakness of ego controls.

> Of considerable importance . . . is the strength and operation of the individual's ego controls—that is, his ability to control and regulate the expression of personal needs, anxieties, and defenses in order to prevent them from distorting his effort to appraise situations realistically and deal with them effectively.[135]

Where ego controls are strong, George suggests, an actor might still be able to hold in check the political expression of strong personal needs, if he perceived that the situation militated against such expression.

While for some compulsives, the power of the superego, driving them on to do the moral thing, would be too powerful for the ego's reality testing to do much good, other compulsives, with stronger ego controls, might be able to turn off the process of rigidification before it went too far.

The case of Joseph McCarthy, however, seems clearly to present a man who had virtually no ego controls at all available to him—at least in the political sphere. For McCarthy, there seems to have been nothing available to bring about the control of impulses that saves most people from one kind of disaster or another. Yet McCarthy's self-defeating behavior differs considerably from that of the compulsives who engage in such behavior.

To put the matter in Freudian terms, the compulsives' weakness of ego controls allow them to become dominated by the harsh and unyielding demands of the superego. The reality testing functions of the ego that might be expected to introduce rational calculations into their thought are forced to take a backseat to the internal, moralistic compulsions of the superego.

In the case of the impulsive, however, the weakness of the ego results instead in surrender to the flood of demands made by the id—the pleasure-seeking component of the human psyche. Thus, the impulsive finds little resistance from either the superego or the ego to doing what he wishes to do at the moment. Neither morality nor cognition stand in the way of the impulsive's immediate gratification of his urges. The compulsive "must" act as he does; the impulsive simply "cannot help it." Here, the Machiavellian stands in strong contrast, for despite relatively low concern for the conventional morality that the superego might represent, the high Mach's strong ego controls allow him the measure of reality testing that is necessary for long-range success. The impulsive has nothing comparable to prevent him from ultimately pushing too far and defeating himself.

Having stepped for a moment into Freudian terminology, one can perhaps benefit from considering McCarthy's political socialization in terms more Freudian than has been the norm in political science. Specifically, it has been suggested that political socialization has something of a dual nature.

> First, it entails the closing off of certain behavioral options. An initially wide range of alternative behaviors is narrowed radically as one is socialized. Second, socialization serves to "make one social" as it opens up and develops the individual, providing him or her with an array of social identities and relationships.[136]

It is the latter aspect of socialization that has been the focus of most attention by political scientists. Perhaps the former aspect is deserving of equally careful study.

The notion of "closing off" behavioral options derives its theoretical underpinnings from the Freudian conception of socialization as a taming of the child's wild, natural impulses toward immediate gratification. This element of socialization has perhaps received less attention than the ways in which children acquire political knowledge and attitudes—ways in which they are made "social." Too rarely has the question been asked: "How does political socialization control the natural antipolitical predispositions of the child?"[137] In the apparent failure of political socialization in the fundamentally antipolitical Joe McCarthy, perhaps one can begin to glimpse at least the outline of a possible answer to that question.

## Notes

1. See Lasswell, *Psychopathology and Politics,* pp. 74–76.

2. Barber, *Presidential Character,* pp. 7–8.

3. George, "Assessing Presidential Character," p. 245. Another emphasis has been on the "operational code" guiding political behavior. See Nathan Leites, *The Operational Code of the Politburo* (New York: McGraw-Hill, 1951). A useful approach to the study of belief systems in childhood is Jeanne Knutson's concept of "prepolitical ideology." See her "Prepolitical Ideologies."

4. Milton Rokeach, *The Open and Closed Mind* (New York: Basic Books, 1960), p. 33.

5. Giovanni Sartori, "Politics, Ideology, and Belief Systems," *American Political Science Review* 63 (June 1969): 400.

6. George, "Assessing Presidential Character," p. 245.

7. Robert Putnam, *The Beliefs of Politicians* (New Haven: Yale University Press, 1973), p. 3.

8. Lasswell, *Psychopathology and Politics,* p. 262.

9. On power seeking as compensation for childhood deprivations, see Lasswell, *Power and Personality* pp. 39–40.

10. Ibid., chap. 4.

11. George and George, *Wilson and House.*

12. Ibid., p. 320.

13. Barber, *Lawmakers;* idem, *Presidential Character.*

14. Barber, *Lawmakers,* pp. 85–86.

15. Barber, *Presidential Character,* pp. 97–98.

16. Barber, *Lawmakers,* p. 90.

17. Barber, *Presidential Character,* pp. 12–13. Katz, "Patterns of Leadership," suggests that the active-negative category is severely strained when a "perfectionistic conscience" is found not only for Woodrow Wilson and Herbert Hoover, but also for Lyndon Johnson and Richard Nixon.

18. This lack of a need to rationalize his behavior also sets McCarthy apart from Robert Tucker's "neurotic personality" (rooted in the work of Karen Horney), and from Lloyd Etheredge's "narcissistic personality" (derived from the ideas of Heinz Kohut). Both types are characterized by the simultaneous presence of high and low self-estimates, so that an idealized self is fantasized. The failure of the empirical self to live up to the image of the idealized self generates a powerful intrapsychic conflict not evident in the case of Joe McCarthy. See Robert C. Tucker, "The Georges' Wilson Reconsidered: An Essay on Psycho-biography," *American Political Science Review* 71 (June 1977): 606–18; and Lloyd Etheredge, "Hardball Politics: A Model," *Political Psychology* 1 (Spring 1979): 3–26.

19. Rovere, *Senator Joe McCarthy,* p. 58.

20. Bayley, *McCarthy and the Press,* pp. 67, 68, 70.

21. Ibid., p. 150.

22. James A. Wechsler, *Reflections of an Angry Middle-Aged Editor* (New York: Random House, 1960), p. 177.

23. Rovere, *Senator Joe McCarthy,* p. 253.

24. Potter, *Days of Shame* p. 21.

25. Rovere, *Senator Joe McCarthy,* p. 72.

26. Paul Wilkes, "Leonard Boudin: The Left's Lawyer's Layer," *New York Times Magazine,* 14 November 1971, p. 53.

27. Allan Nevins, *Herbert H. Lehman and His Era* (New York: Charles Scribner's Sons, 1963), p. 436.

28. Griffith, *Politics of Fear,* p. 14.

29. Rovere, *Senator Joe McCarthy,* pp. 54–55; Thomas, *When Even Angels Wept,* p. 237; Cook, *Nightmare Decade,* p. 76.

30. Rovere, *Senator Joe McCarthy,* p. 57.

31. Ibid., p. 55.

32. Bayley, *McCarthy and the Press,* p. 36.

33. Rovere, *Senator Joe McCarthy,* p. 58.

34. Bayley, *McCarthy and the Press,* p. 150.

35. Griffith, *Politics of Fear,* p. 15.

36. Bayley, *McCarthy and the Press,* p. 150.

37. Reeves, *Life and Times,* p. 287.

38. Griffith, "Notorious Baiter," p. 57.

39. Reeves, *Life and Times,* p. 235.

40. Cohn, *McCarthy,* pp. 9–10.

41. O'Brien, *McCarthyism in Wisconsin,* p. 90; Reeves, *Life and Times,* p. 199.

42. Bayley, *McCarthy and the Press,* p. 73.

43. Ibid., p. 150.

44. Rovere, *Senator Joe McCarthy,* p. 58.

45. Reeves, *Life and Times,* pp. 287–90. Oshinsky, *Conspiracy So Immense,* suggests that a conversion may have taken place in March 1953, after the Voice of America hearings (p. 285).

46. This suggestion is made by Eric F. Goldman in his review of Reeves, *Life and Times*, (see "The Rise of a Demagogue," *New York Times Book Review*, 11 April 1982, p. 19.

47. Earl Latham, *The Communist Controversy in Washington: From the New Deal to McCarthy* (Cambridge: Harvard University Press, 1966), pp. 3–4.

48. Rovere, *Senator Joe McCarthy*, p. 60 (emphasis in original).

49. Rorty and Decter, *McCarthy and Communists*, p. 150.

50. Ibid., p. 23.

51. Rovere, *Senator Joe McCarthy*, p. 47.

52. Ibid., p. 48.

53. Herberg, "McCarthy and Hitler," p. 15.

54. This corresponds to the emphasis on "genesis" discussed by Greenstein, *Personality and Politics*, pp. 66–67. See the discussion in Chapter 2 above.

55. Faye Crosby and Travis L. Crosby, "Psychobiography and Psychohistory," in *The Handbook of Political Behavior*, vol. 1, ed. Samuel L. Long, (New York: Plenum Press, 1981), p. 219. The concept of coherent whole explanation corresponds roughly to Greenstein's description of "phenomenology" and "dynamics" (see *Personality and Politics*, pp. 65–66).

56. Herberg, "McCarthy and Hitler," pp. 14–15.

57. Reeves, *Life and Times*, p. 18.

58. Ibid., p. 67.

59. Ibid., p. 245.

60. Rovere, *Senator Joe McCarthy*, p. 241.

61. Daniel Bell, ed., *The New American Right* (New York: Criterion, 1955).

62. Rogin, *Intellectuals and McCarthy*, p. 228.

63. Ibid., p. 231.

64. Philip Converse, "The Nature of Belief Systems in Mass Publics," in *Ideology and Discontent*, ed. David E. Apter (New York: Free Press, 1964), p. 207.

65. W. Lance Bennett, *Public Opinion in American Politics* (New York: Harcourt Brace Jovanovich, 1980), pp. 48–49.

66. Fred I. Greenstein, "Personality and Politics," in *Handbook of Political Science*, vol. 2, ed. Fred I. Greenstein and Nelson W. Polsby, (Reading, Mass.: Addison-Wesley, 1975), p. 9.

67. R. W. Connell, *The Child's Construction of Politics* (Melbourne: Melbourne University Press, 1971), p. 18.

68. Rovere, *Senator Joe McCarthy*, p. 46.

69. Bayley, *McCarthy and the Press*, pp. 75, 29; Samuel Shaffer, *On and Off the Floor* (New York: Newsweek Books, 1980), p. 31.

70. Bayley, *McCarthy and the Press*, p. 68.

71. Rovere, *Senator Joe McCarthy*, p. 168.

72. Reeves, *Life and Times*, pp. 227–29.

73. Rovere, *Senator Joe McCarthy*, pp. 132–33.

74. Ibid., pp. 112–18.

75. Margaret Chase Smith with William C. Lewis, *Declaration of Conscience* (Garden City, N.Y.: Doubleday, 1972), p. 7.

76. Rovere, *Senator Joe McCarthy*, pp. 169–70 (emphasis in original).

77. Reeves, *Life and Times*, p. 401.

78. Rovere, *Senator Joe McCarthy*, pp. 133–34.

79. Reeves, *Life and Times*, p. 237.

80. Rovere, *Senator Joe McCarthy*, pp. 178–79.

81. Reeves, *Life and Times*, p. 374.

82. James T. Patterson, *Mr. Republican: A Biography of Robert A. Taft* (Boston: Houghton Mifflin, 1972), p. 503.

83. Rovere, *Senator Joe McCarthy*, p. 195.

84. Sartori, "Politics, Ideology, and Belief Systems."

85. Ibid., p. 403.

86. Ibid., p. 405.

87. Ibid.

88. Reeves, *Life and Times*, p. 8.

89. Ibid., p. 288.

90. O'Brien, *McCarthyism in Wisconsin*, p. 23.

91. Ibid., pp. 36, 38–39.

92. Ibid., p. 39.

93. Sartori, "Politics, Ideology, and Belief Systems," p. 405 (emphasis added).

94. See, for example, Robert Axelrod, ed., *Structure of Decision: The Cognitive Maps of Political Elites* (Princeton: Princeton University Press, 1976).

95. Converse, "Belief Systems."

96. Richard Christie and Florence L. Geis, *Studies in Machiavellianism* (New York: Academic Press, 1970). See also Florence Geis, "Machiavellianism," in *Dimensions of Personality,* ed. Harvey London and J. E. Exner, Jr., (New York: Wiley, 1978), pp. 305–63.

97. Shaffer, *On and Off the Floor,* p. 26.

98. Bayley, *McCarthy and the Press,* p. 151.

99. Cohn, *McCarthy,* p. 269.

100. O'Brien, *McCarthyism in Wisconsin*, p. 17.

101. Richard M. Merelman, "The Development of Political Ideology: A Framework for the Analysis of Political Socialization," *American Political Science Review* 63 (September 1969): 750–67.

102. Barber, "Predicting Presidential Styles," pp. 52–53.

103. George, "Assessing Presidential Character," p. 243.

104. Jerome Kagan, H. A. Moss, and I. E. Siegel, "Psychological Significance of Styles of Conceptualization," in *Basic Cognitive Processes,* ed. J. C. Wright and Jerome Kagan, Monographs of the Society for Research in Child Development, 28, no. 2 (1963); Jerome Kagan, Bernice L. Rosman, Deborah Day, Joseph Albert, and William Phillips, "Information Processing in the Child: Significance of Analytic and Reflective Attitudes," *Psychological Monographs: General and Applied* 78 (1964); Jerome Kagan, "Impulsive and Reflective Children," in *Learning and the Educational Process,* ed. J. Krumboltz (Chicago: Rand-McNally, 1965), pp. 133–61; Jerome Kagan, Leslie Pearson, and Lois Welch, "Conceptual Impulsivity and Inductive Reasoning," *Child Development* 37 (1966): 583–94; Jerome Kagan, "Developmental Studies in Reflection and Analysis," in *Perceptual Development in Children,* ed. Aline H. Kidd and Jeanne L. Riviere, (New York: International Universities Press, 1966), pp. 487–522.

105. David Shapiro, *Neurotic Styles* (New York: Basic Books, 1965).

106. Kagan, "Developmental Studies in Reflection and Analysis," p. 488.

107. Ibid.

108. Kagan et al., "Information Processing in the Child," p. 33.

109. Shapiro, *Neurotic Styles,* p. 134.

110. Ibid., p. 139.

111. Ibid., pp. 139–40.

112. Ibid., p. 143.

113. Bayley, *McCarthy and the Press,* pp. 150, 156; Potter, *Days of Shame,* p. 21; Rovere, *Senator Joe McCarthy,* p. 134.

114. O'Brien, *McCarthyism in Wisconsin,* p. 184.

115. Ibid., pp. 16–17; Griffith, *Politics of Fear,* p. 16; Reeves, *Life and Times,* p. 28.

116. Shaffer, *On and Off the Floor,* p. 25.

117. Thomas, *When Even Angels Wept,* p. 202.

118. Edward Bennett Williams, *One Man's Freedom* (New York: Atheneum, 1962), p. 61.

119. Cohn, *McCarthy,* p. 275.

120. Reeves, *Life and Times,* p. 15.

121. Barber, *Presidential Character,* p. 97.

122. Quoted in Shapiro, *Neurotic Styles,* p. 146.

123. Ibid., p. 151.

124. Ibid., pp. 149–50.

125. Ibid., p. 154.

126. Ibid., p. 150.

127. Rovere, *Senator Joe McCarthy,* p. 140.

128. Bayley, *McCarthy and the Press*, p. 75.
129. Shapiro, *Neurotic Styles*, p. 143.
130. Ibid., p. 147.
131. Ibid.
132. Rovere, *Senator Joe McCarthy*, p. 60.
133. Ibid.
134. George and George, *Wilson and House*, pp. 320–21.
135. George, "Assessing Presidential Character," p. 253.
136. Richard E. Dawson, Kenneth Prewitt, and Karen S. Dawson, *Political Socialization*, 2d ed. (Boston: Little, Brown, 1977), p. 36.
137. Ibid.

# 5
## McCarthy's Political Belief System: Development

### Cognitive Aspects of the Political World

In the previous chapter, the nature of Joe McCarthy's political belief system was examined. There, the emphasis was on *phenomenology* and *dynamics*—the characteristics and functioning of that belief system. I turn now to the issue of *genesis*—the origins of McCarthy's vision of the political world. Here, one necessarily stands upon less than firm ground in seeking relevant evidence about McCarthy's childhood, and in trying to make sense of that evidence. As Fred Greenstein has noted, "explanations of genesis are perhaps most likely to be controversial."[1]

[I]n practice the paucity of satisfactorily detailed and verified observations of developmental experience reduces the chances of widely accepted genetic explanations. Furthermore, genetic explanations are weakened because there is still imperfect knowledge of general principles of human development, and because many of the more interesting genetic hypotheses posit relationships that are in principle likely to be weak, or at any rate complex and difficult to document—relationships between phenomena remote from one another in time and connected by many mediating links.[2]

The difficulty of the enterprise, however, does not make the effort less worthwhile or less interesting. So long as one does not forget the limitations imposed by the nature of the evidence with which one is dealing, there is nothing to be lost by pushing as far as possible in seeking out the nature of the developmental processes that may have shaped Joseph McCarthy's political personality.

How do people develop a world view, or a political belief system? Clearly the process called political socialization is at the heart of any answer to such a question.[3] In the course of growing up, children are exposed to the political culture of those around them, particularly to the political attitudes and values of their family, peer groups, schools, and mass media. Through a complex series of processes, such bits and pieces of information, opinions, and values are used by the child to "construct" for himself or herself a mental picture of the political world. It is this mental picture that permits the growing child to interpret and make sense of what occurs in the realm of politics.

To some extent, the process of political socialization can be compared to other, more general processes of childhood socialization. Particularly relevant here are the two dimensions of *cognitive* and *moral* development, which can be used to relate the child to the political world in the form of two broad questions: (1) What *is* the political world? (cognition), and (2) What *should be* my relationship to it? (morality).

R. W. Connell has outlined the basis of a model for the development of political beliefs that, in general terms, traces the child's movement toward answers to these questions.[4] Connell follows the course of a child's development of political beliefs along two broad dimensions. First, the dimension of *Interpretations* delineates the path a child must travel in order to understand what politics is, how it differs from the rest of the world, and how it works.[5] The emphasis here is on understanding the political world in ever more sophisticated, realistic, and coherent terms. Connell's second dimension, *Stances,* is a more subjectively oriented one, and appears more concerned with moral than with cognitive growth (although the two can never be fully separated).[6] Here, the task of the maturing child is seen as the adoption of a personal stance toward the political world. The child must ask himself what politics means and what his own relationship ought to be to that world of politics. Along this dimension, the movement is toward an understanding of politics as being conflictual.

Once past that stage, the child must come to comprehend the underlying basis of such conflict.

> The younger children do not represent conflict in the political world as conflict over issues. The gradual mastering of this form of political conflict in late childhood and early adolescence is particularly interesting. Conflict over issues involves debate over alternative policies, and understanding issue-conflict requires a grasp of the idea of a policy.[7]

To understand politics solely as conflict, with no policy-rooted rationale, is not to understand politics at all, nor the point of one's relationship to it. To the extent that policy thinking does occur (usually by middle adolescence), however, it sets the stage for an understanding of politics in terms of advocacy of group interests, and perhaps even ideologies. By the last stage of this developmental process, if development of interpretations (knowledge of politics) has kept pace with the maturing of stances (judgment in politics), the stage of ideological thought has been reached, and the child (now, more properly, a young adult) has developed an important and complex tool for understanding and acting in the political world.

What must now be stressed, of course, is the actual difficulty involved for a child as he moves along the paths so far described. It is clear that, in

TABLE 4
STAGES IN THE DEVELOPMENT OF POLITICAL BELIEF

| INTERPRETATIONS | | STANCES | | |
|---|---|---|---|---|
| *Stage* | *Characteristics* | *Stage* | | *Characteristics* |
| 1. Intuitive thinking | Confusion of political and nonpolitical material; wild leaps in narrative and argument; fantasy | 1. Politics not problematic | | Most judgments ad hoc, unqualified, not consistent. A few stable attitudes formed under adult instruction |
| 2. Primitive realism | Disappearance of fantasy; identification of a distinct political world at a remove from the self; appearance of task pool | | | |
| 3. Construction of political order | Division of task pool; expansion of concrete detail about politics; perception of the multiple relationships among political actors | 2. Politics problematic | (i) isolated stances | (a) Positions taken on issues; preferences expressed |
| 4. Ideological thinking | Use of abstract terms in political argument; conceptions of societies and polities as wholes | | (ii) Interconnected stances | (b) Alternative actions considered and sometimes undertaken |
| | | Ideologies | | |

SOURCE: Connell, *Child's Construction of Politics,* p. 231.

real life, few people ever actually attain the stage of ideological thinking. Fixation at some prior stage of development is by far the likelier event. The path to ideology is not an easy one, and it is important to understand why this should be so.

Connell's explanation for this phenomenon focuses upon the separability of the political world from the rest of the child's universe of experience. In particular, he sharply differentiates between general cognitive development and cognitive development regarding the world of politics. Intellectual growth in general is viewed as following the model of cognitive development outlined by Jean Piaget, and results from the maturational growth of cognitive capacities in the child combined with opportunities for interaction with his environment. The child must come to understand the meaning of objects, space, time, and causality in order to be able to function in the world. Cognitive development consists of coming to an increasingly mature and more accurate conception of these aspects of reality. In broad outline, Piaget describes the following stages:

*Sensorimotor stage (birth–2 years).* The infant comes to distinguish itself from other objects, locates itself in space, begins to determine the substantiality and permanence of objects, and develops the beginnings of an ability to manipulate symbols.

*Preoperational stage (2–7 years).* The child accepts his world at face value, and while he may begin to classify objects, can usually do so only on the basis of one dimension. The ability to think in symbolic terms grows, although the child still remains more intuitive than logical in his thought. This is the egocentric period in which the child tends to interpret his world almost entirely in terms of its effect upon him.

*Stage of concrete operations (7–11 years).* At about this time the movement toward logical thought begins, and the child develops the ability to reason. Abstract thought, however, still remains unlikely during this stage, and the focus of thought is very much on concrete objects.

*Stage of formal operations (11–15 years).* The final period of cognitive development finds the child now able to think logically even about abstract verbal propositions and relationships. Cause and effect, the fundamental basis of scientific thought, should now be within his realm of understanding.[8]

For Piaget and developmental psychologists, the stages described above represent an *invariant* sequence, through which every child must pass in order to attain the level of genuinely mature thought. It is impossible, in this view, to move to any stage without having passed first through the ones preceding it. Thus, for the maturing child, one can posit a normal development taking it from a point at birth where it is unaware even of itself, through a stage where all that occurs is interpreted in strictly egocentric terms, and finally to a point where the child develops sufficient empathy to be able to imagine itself in another's position. Paralleling this movement beyond egocentric thought is the movement toward causal thinking, in which the child ceases to see events as random and unconnected, and begins to develop a coherent picture of how the world functions. It is, of course, quite possible for a child to become fixated at one of the earlier stages of development, and various forms of cognitive damage or underdevelopment are not uncommon.

Connell's model of the development of political beliefs can be seen to follow, in broad outline at least, Piaget's framework of analysis. In the realm of Interpretations, one finds stages labeled "intuitive thinking" and "primitive realism," which parallel quite closely Piaget's preoperational stage and stage of concrete operations, respectively. "Construction of political order" can be regarded either as a bridging of the stage of concrete operations and that of formal operations, or as the beginning of the formal operations stage. Finally, "ideological thinking" can be seen as paralleling the "scientific" thinking associated with the stage of formal operations. Thus, it might seem, at first glance, that one ought to be able to engage in some wholesale borrowing from the developmental psychologists in order to understand the development of a person's political thought. But this is where the concept of separability enters, for the political world of the child does not come to be "constructed" in quite so direct a fashion as the rest of the universe.[9]

Important distinctions must be made between the child's physical universe, his immediate social universe, and the more distant political universe. A child is likeliest to learn the reality of his physical universe and least likely to understand his political universe. In the realm of the physical, it should be evident, the subject matter that is to be learned is immediately present and is in tangible form. Hot and cold, hard and soft, dull and sharp are qualities the testing of which provides immediate feedback enabling the child to validate his conceptions of the physical world. In learning about this world, the rewards and punishments come quickly, and reinforcement is immediate. In the sphere of politics, however, the objects of the child's thoughts are not immediately accessible. Both objectively and subjectively, they are far removed from the child, and this, of necessity, drastically alters the manner in which the child learns about them. He *feels* remote from the political world, and in fact, of course, he *is* remote from it. He is unable to validate his conceptions of politics.

Moreover, the very stuff with which the child must work in trying to construct his picture of the political world consists of adult thought forms.

The physical world, of course, provides no such obstacles and the child is therefore free to exercise his mental abilities to the extent he is capable. But the political world is already, to begin with, a social construct, defined by adults in adult terms. Unlike Piaget's paradigm for the child's construction of his physical universe, therefore, one finds in the political universe that the child is faced with the task of attaining adult modes of thought, not through direct construction independent of adults and their concepts, but with materials manufactured and supplied by adults.

To some extent, the same complexities can be glimpsed in the child's attempt to orient himself within his immediate social world, but here at least, the response of parents, peers, and school offer the relatively quick feedback that helps the child to know whether his understanding of this world is right or wrong. Parents, for example, are likely to be greatly concerned that a child come to understand their authority and their approval or disapproval of specific actions. Because a proper understanding of the immediate social world of the child is so closely linked to his proper behavior within it, the child is likely to learn about that world relatively quickly.

The political world, on the other hand, differs in important respects from the picture painted above. Parents, for example, may be relatively uninterested in politics, and where that is the case, the chances may increase that the child will come to hold erroneous or deviant notions about politics. If politics is unimportant to a child's parents, then the child's learning about politics will not be very important to them. The child may then quite easily pick up myths and misconceptions about politics that may persist throughout life. To cite but one example, such a child might come to an understanding of politics as conflict, but might never move on to comprehend the policy basis of such conflict. With no tangible or easily ascertainable standard against which to measure his immature conception, there would be little opportunity for a mature vision of politics to develop.

Thus, it would seem to be the case that in developing a sense of what the political sphere is all about, the child has the worst of two worlds. On the one hand, he cannot directly construct his own interpretations based upon direct experience (because adults and *their* mental constructs get in between him and the political world). Yet at the same time, the child may receive relatively little aid from those adults in determining whether the conceptions he does develop are correct (in the sense of according with the societal consensus). Taking into account, therefore, the complexities involved in the process of learning about politics, it becomes easier to understand how a child might develop ideas about politics that become the root of unusual, even deviant, political styles. People able to function perfectly well in the everyday world (in its physical and social manifestations) might nonetheless carry about with them quite bizarre conceptions of the political world.

Following Connell's line of thought about the separability of the political universe, it seems reasonable to suggest that a child could quite easily remain so isolated from political thinking that his ideas about politics would be highly unintegrated, even chaotic. Those ideas about politics would very likely also be poorly related to the child's thinking about other facets of his life. Indeed, there are probably large numbers of people who fit this description very well. Philip Converse's seminal article, "The Nature of Belief Systems in Mass Publics"—a key pluralist text—argues precisely that most people do not think about politics in a structured and coherent way.[10] An important general question that arises from such a conclusion concerns the effects upon democratic government when the average person is incapable of systematic thought about politics. More immediately relevant for the present purpose is the question of the impact of such a style of political belief when it is that of a major American political figure rather than of members of the mass public.

## McCarthy's Political World

To what extent can McCarthy's childhood background be regarded as one likely to produce a fragmented and confused picture of the political world? To what extent can it be shown that for McCarthy, there was only a limited and distorted understanding of the purposes of politics? To what extent can McCarthy's unusual political style be productively viewed as fostered by his particular political belief system?

Returning for a moment to Harold Lasswell's interpretation of political man, it might be profitable to examine for a moment the $d$ factor in his equation. Lasswell spoke of "displacement upon public objects," and perhaps the time has come to treat this variable in the same way that private motives ($p$) and the processes of rationalization in terms of the public interest ($r$) routinely have been. The latter two have been viewed in terms of a broad range of variability, and perhaps it is time now to ask in what ways the displacement process itself may vary.

The grossest variation, which Lasswell of course noted, was simply whether such displacement took place at all.[11] Such variation distinguished political man from nonpolitical man, for without displacement there could be no political man. But even within the category of political man, it seems logical to assume that more subtle variations might exist, and that these could play an important role in shaping political styles. "Public objects" may after all, assume many different forms in the perceptions of different people. Lasswell noted, for example, that "agitators differ appreciably in the specificity or generality of the social objects upon which they succeed in displacing their affects."[12] Agitators who had been resentful of their parents tended to focus upon immediate and personal objects in the environment, while those who had been consciously attached to their parents were likelier to choose remote and general objects.

Perhaps another important dimension along which such variability could occur might be a moral one. Politics might be seen by some as primarily an arena for the attainment of moral goals, by others as mainly providing an opportunity for personal economic and social gain, and by still others as no more than a highly entertaining game.[13] Thus, childhood views of politics could reasonably be expected to play a significant role in determining just how people come to view the world of politics and its purposes.

In this respect, Joseph McCarthy's childhood is striking because of the apparently total absence of any links at all to the world of politics. McCarthy, in his early life, appears from all the available evidence to have displayed virtually no political awareness or concern. Unlike most of those who become political activists, McCarthy's childhood and adolescence were singularly barren of any political content. The McCarthys were not a particularly political family, and of Joe McCarthy it could only be concluded that

> his roots in Democratic politics were shallow, a matter of ethnic tradition and environment. . . . Two of McCarthy's uncles—the only two whose politics are known—had been Democrats. McCarthy's father had also been a Democrat, though apparently not an avid one; Stephen McCarthy, oldest of the McCarthy boys, could not recall that his father had ever discussed the subject.[14]

As noted earlier, McCarthy's "interest in and commitment to political thought ran no deeper than the prejudices of Tim and Bid."[15]

Moreover, if McCarthy and his parents were Democrats in the Wisconsin of the 1920s, it is perhaps not at all farfetched to suggest that, in a very real sense, they were virtually outside of politics anyway. Students of political history know that the political battles of that day in Wisconsin were largely fought between Republicans and Progressives, with Democrats running a very weak third most of the time. There is no evidence that McCarthy or his family had any particular interest in Wisconsin politics, and their Democratic allegiance could account for this. Certainly it is worth noting that there is absolutely no clue as to what McCarthy might have felt about Robert La Follette, the dominant figure in Wisconsin's politics from the late 1890s to 1925, when he died. Unlike Wayne Morse, a later Senate colleague, who grew up in Wisconsin at approximately the same time as McCarthy, and who, as a schoolboy, was completely caught up in the battles of Progressive politics, there is simply no evidence that La Follette had any meaning for McCarthy or that politics was of any significance to him until he was well into his twenties.[16] One can search, with equally barren results, for the slightest hint that McCarthy or his family were in any way affected by the candidacy for president of Al Smith, the first Catholic nominee, and Irish to boot.

How could McCarthy have come to maturity with so little awareness of, or concern for, politics? The answer must lie in the processes of political socialization that help the child to construct a political universe for himself. In McCarthy's case, it seems clear, the agents of political socialization failed to create any real linkages to the world of politics. McCarthy's parents appear not to have been interested in talking about politics (indeed, if one accepts Anderson and May's portrait, Timothy McCarthy was not interested in talking at all). McCarthy's situation may therefore have been quite different from that of the average American politician coming out of a middle-class or upper-class home where issues of government and politics would be far more likely to be discussed.

It is unlikely that children in their preteen years learn a great deal about politics from their peers, but to the extent that they do, McCarthy may have been isolated in this respect also. If one were to accept Anderson and May's picture of McCarthy's poor relationships with his older brothers, and of rather sporadic and weak interaction with children his own age, McCarthy would have to be seen as cut off from his peers. But even if one were to accept the view that McCarthy's childhood was a normal one, it still seems likely that among the children of the Irish settlers in Outagamie County—Democrats in a Republican time and place—politics might have seemed even more distant and irrelevant than it normally does to children. And by leaving school at the age of fourteen, McCarthy may have cut himself off from any avenues of political learning that might have existed in formal education. Nor could cramming four years of high school into one year at the age of nineteen have done much to enhance a mature vision of politics and government in America.

Finally, of course, one can think of the mass media as substitute teachers for those deprived of other modes of political socialization. Today, for example, television may provide a window on politics even for those growing up in an otherwise apolitical environment. In the 1920s, of course, television did not exist, and the impact of the mass media was consequently neither so intense nor so pervasive as it is today. Radio was in its infancy and primarily a medium of entertainment; newspapers in rural Wisconsin probably had little impact on children beyond their comic strips and sports pages.

Thus, it should not be too surprising to find McCarthy entering the political arena with little more than a nominal partisan identification. Though he was a strong supporter of FDR, a friend would later remark, "I can't say that he really believed in what Roosevelt stood for."[17] When expediency later demanded it, McCarthy had no hesitation about dropping his Democratic label. In 1936, he had run for district attorney as a Democrat; by 1944, he was running for the Senate as a Republican. The switch was clearly no more than a straightforward concession to the realities of office seeking in the Wisconsin of the 1940s. It was an advantage, as McCarthy himself later acknowledged, being "a Republican with a Democratic name."[18]

Clearly, McCarthy's childhood was one that had infused little sense of politics and purpose. To the extent that political ideas must be mediated through various adult socializing agents, McCarthy had been cut off from such ideas. It is important to stress, however, that there is nothing very unusual about such a background; what is somewhat unusual is that someone from it would go on to become a major actor in the American political arena.

### Moral Aspects of the Political World

R. W. Connell's picture of the development of *stances* to politics paralleling the development of *interpretations* of politics points to the important role moral development plays in the growth of ideological thought. The growth of ideology in a person calls not just for an understanding of how the world of politics is constituted (cognitive knowledge), but also for the adoption of a personal stance toward that world (moral judgment). These two components of ideology have been noted for years by political scientists who have, in general, chosen to emphasize one or the other in their studies.

Philip Converse, as noted in the previous chapter, has tended to focus upon the cognitive aspects, defining ideology as a belief system characterized by high constraint, great range, and a centrality of political ideas.[19] The key word here seems to be *constraint,* and Converse defines this in terms of a logical interconnectedness of political ideas such that knowledge of a person's political attitudes toward some matters enables accurate prediction of his other political attitudes. Ideology, in this scheme, is rooted in cognitive sophistication, and the inability of the masses to attain such a level of sophistication makes impossible their attainment of the level of ideological thought.

A second strand of thought regarding ideology has tended to stress its normative-evaluative aspects, focusing more upon content than structure, and emphasizing its ethical and moral nature. Robert Lane, in particular, has been associated with this view that ideologies "are normative, ethical, moral in tone and content."[20] What seems clear, of course, is that ideology can best be understood in terms of *both* its cognitive and moral strands. The truth of this is quickly understood when one realizes that in the theories of developmental psychologists like Piaget, cognitive and moral development are intimately linked together in a reinforcing pattern. Thus, in order to understand the failure to develop ideology, one cannot look at its cognitive dimensions as though these existed in a vacuum. The impact of moral development processes must be subjected to equal scrutiny.

It is the work of Richard Merelman on the birth of ideology in individuals that proves most useful for undertaking an analysis of the moral underpinnings of ideology. In order to think ideologically, Merelman argues,

a person must: 1) have cognitive skills which allow him to see linkages between ideas and events. Such linkages determine the amount of constraint in his belief system. 2) Have a developed morality which allows him to evaluate consistently the ethical meanings of political events.[21]

Moreover, "the development of cognitive skills and the construction of a conscience are reinforcing processes. Laying the groundwork for ideology is all of a piece."[22] At the same time that cognitive growth enables the child to realize that inanimate objects do not have a life of their own and that there is no invariant divine order controlling events, he comes to realize the extent to which humans can control their destinies. This cognitive growth enables the child to comprehend the extent to which there are choices and possibilities in the moral sphere, and that here again, humans are in control. Cognitive immaturity, in other words, would be likely to prevent an understanding of the complexities of moral choice, and would hamper moral growth. In order to understand more fully the actual processes at work in moral development, Merelman turns to the work of Jean Piaget and of Lawrence Kohlberg.[23]

Piaget, in the 1930s, began to develop a framework for the analysis of moral growth in scientific rather than normative terms. By focusing not upon the *content* of a moral judgment, but upon the *standards* by which it was arrived at (that is, universality, inclusiveness, consistency, and impersonality), morality could be seen as developing from its primitive stages in childhood to the relative maturity possible in adulthood.[24] This development, moreover, tended, at least in rough outline, to parallel the growth of cognitive development, and a series of stages could be discerned that were somewhat analogous to the stages of cognitive growth. Piaget saw three broad stages of the child's moral development:

*Morality of obedience.* The child has no sense of right and wrong, and responds only to punishment to prevent "bad" behavior. There are no internalized restraints within the child, and it can be viewed as functioning amorally (really, premorally).

*Moral realism.* The child confuses moral laws with physical rules, regarding them as fixed, eternal, and beyond human control. Parents and adults are seen as all-knowing, and their handing down of moral laws means they are sacred and beyond challenge. In relations with peers, concepts of reciprocity begin to emerge, and justice is seen as important. A morality of cooperation develops, in which the child does "right" in order to get along with others.

*Moral autonomy.* The child comes to develop a sense of moral laws as serving human purposes and values, and behaves morally in order to conform to his own standards of right and wrong. A moral sense is now internalized within the child, and no longer requires the exertion of external forces to keep him in check.[25]

In recent years, Piaget's framework has been expanded and elaborated in the work of Lawrence Kohlberg, who has created a six-stage analysis of the process of moral development:

Level I. Premoral

    Stage 1: Punishment and obedience orientation
    Stage 2. Naive instrumental hedonism

Level II. Morality of conventional role conformity

    Stage 3. Good-boy morality of maintaining good relations, approval
           by others
    Stage 4: Authority-maintaining morality

Level III. Morality of self-accepted moral principles

    Stage 5. Morality of contract, of individual rights, and of demo-
           cratically accepted law
    Stage 6. Morality of individual principles of conscience[26]

Each separate stage finds a person behaving correctly from a somewhat different base of justification. In broad terms, the movement from lower to higher stages of morality is one from right behavior in order to avoid punishment to right behavior in order to avoid self-condemnation. The child, as he matures, comes increasingly to realize that he cannot simply rely upon "the world" (that is, his immediate environment) to judge his actions for him. If he is to grow up, he must move from a mere yielding to punishments and sanctions imposed by his parents (a morality of restraint), to doing the right thing because he must get along with others (a morality of cooperation), and finally to acting properly because he lives by certain self-accepted standards (moral autonomy). The process of developing a conscience can thus be seen as one in which a person acquires a moral compass to guide his behavior in the world. As a child, moral choices are relatively easy; one does as one pleases until the world (usually in the form of parents) closes in to administer punishment. "Because the world is itself reliable and can substitute its own controls," remarks Merelman, "the child does not need the judgmental consistency which conscience provides him."[27] But as one grows up, the process of choice becomes harder and harder as more and more of the moral burden is placed upon the individual. Yet without that ability to make one's own moral judgments, it becomes impossible to conceive of ideology developing.

As with cognitive development, moral development as described by stage theorists like Piaget and Kohlberg must follow an invariant sequence. No stage can be skipped as one climbs to the higher levels of morality, so that unless one attains at some point Piaget's second stage—the morality of cooperation—one can never attain the final stage of moral autonomy. Thus, as with cognitive development, fixation at a stage is possible, although Piaget "expects the autonomous morality of justice to develop in all children, unless development is fixated by unusual coerciveness of parents or cultures or by deprivation of experiences of peer cooperation."[28] Therefore, "Piaget's theory is probably best understood as an ideal type. People must pass through the stages he describes if they are to think ideologically, but most people do not succeed in making the passage."[29] The question then becomes what factors are responsible for determining whether the process of moral development will be completed.

"Anaclitic" theories stress the importance of the child's identification with his parents.[30] From this perspective, child-rearing practices that foster such identification are also likeliest to foster the moral development of the child. Of special importance for such child rearing are: (1) nonphysical modes of punishment, (2) parental warmth, and (3) choice of an appropriate time at which the child is expected to display a sense of responsibility.[31] "Other child rearing patterns will lead to a fragmented view of the political world," argues Merelman.[32]

Physical punishment appears to foster the persistence of a morality of obedience, since it suggests to the child that the willingness to absorb pain provides sufficient expiation for wrongdoing. No burden is placed upon the child to formulate a standard of proper behavior. Parental coldness distances the child from his parents and creates little incentive to live up to their standards in order to avoid disappointing or hurting them. Finally, the failure to require at a relatively early age a sense of responsibility absolves the child of any wrongdoing, since he has never been given any reason to feel that his behavior is a matter of concern to him as well as to his parents. Thus, inadequate child-rearing methods tend to inhibit the identification process and hinder the growth of the cognitive skills and moral framework necessary for the development of political ideology.

A second important factor in moral development has to do with the child's opportunity for participation and role taking in peer groups. Moral development does not simply unfold as part of the process of growing older, but is greatly influenced by the child's interaction with others. In addition to cognitive advance, which can be viewed as a necessary but not sufficient condition for moral advance, the chance to deal with others is important in helping one to develop more mature moral standards. Moral development even to the point of role conformity requires an ability to surmount egocentric modes of thought and to be able to view a situation from others' points of view. Only experience in dealing with others provides such exercise. Thus, Lawrence Kohlberg's findings demonstrated that

> middle-class and working-class children seemed to move through the same sequences, but the middle-class children seemed to move faster and farther. Similar but even more striking differences were found between peer-group participators (popular children) and nonparticipators (unpopular children) in the American sample.[33]

Thus one can conclude that the process of moral development is a two-part one, in which "peer-group differences partly arise from, and partly add on to, prior differences in opportunities for role-taking in the child's family."[34] Now, as earlier with the concept of cognitive development, one can turn back to Joe McCarthy's childhood for evidence regarding the nature of his moral development.

## McCarthy's Moral Development

> I've always felt that Joe lived in a different moral universe. He asked himself only two questions: What do I want and how do I get it. Once he got rolling, you had to step aside. It was every man for himself, sort of what anarchy must be like.[35]

The problem of McCarthy's moral development can be approached in two ways. If one accepts the Anderson and May version of McCarthy's childhood, one can easily conclude that his upbringing was precisely of the sort most likely to result in stunted moral development. Alternatively, if one accepts the view that McCarthy's childhood was in no way extraordinary, one can still suggest that a compartmentalization developed and that this allowed him to create a rigid separation between his public and private lives.

Anderson and May suggest that McCarthy was raised by a stern and uncommunicative father, with whom positive identification would have been difficult, and by a mother who shielded him from the burdens of responsibility by her overprotectiveness. McCarthy, it can be suggested, grew up without ever really having to develop the internal steering mechanism that allows a person to judge for himself the difference between right and wrong. A mother who gave warmth without imposing responsibilities, and a father who imposed responsibilities (perhaps prematurely) while withholding warmth, may have done much to damage the young McCarthy's chances for mature moral development. Indeed, the absence of consistent standards shared by the two parents may have made normal progression in the moral sphere close to impossible. A child needs "parents who profess the same values" and thereby "present a fairly consistent picture of themselves to their children, and . . . a single set of ideals for emulation."[36] By confusing the child in regard to what is expected of him, the possibilities for identification diminish even further, and moral confusion is fostered.

Employing Kohlberg's outline, therefore, one might hypothesize that McCarthy's upbringing, in terms of his relationship with his father (as depicted by Anderson and May) would probably have left him fixated at the first stage of moral development—a punishment-and-obedience orientation, in which one expects outside forces to determine the outer limits of permissible behavior. At best, in terms of his relationship with his mother, from whom he might have been able to expect rewards for good behavior, a Stage 2 level of morality—"naive instrumental hedonism"—could be predicted. In either case, McCarthy's moral development would have been stunted.

Continuing with the picture painted by Anderson and May, one would have to conclude that McCarthy would have been unlikely to have attained even the level of a "morality of conventional role conformity," in which one behaves in a manner that will enable one to get along with one's peers. Anderson and May suggest that McCarthy had little interaction with his peers, hiding when company came to the farm and never learning how to play during his school years. Nor were his relations with his older brothers much better (Anderson and May are silent on McCarthy's relationships with his sisters). Never being forced to deal with his peers might well have left McCarthy at a premoral stage of development, in which external sanctions would continue to be his main guides to appropriate behavior.

One could view McCarthy, then, as someone who would do no more than comply with externally imposed rules—and this, only to the extent that there was sufficient force behind them to assure their enforcement. In the same way that McCarthy's father may have relied most heavily upon physical discipline to keep his child in check, McCarthy's fixation at the premoral level would now mean that his actions in the adult world could only be controlled by outside restraints. There was no force *within* Joe McCarthy to hold him back from a course of action he felt impelled to follow. For McCarthy, with no real internal standards to restrain him, behavior was never really a matter of morality or immorality, for these terms had no real meaning for him.

One can reasonably speculate that McCarthy's success in Manawa might have raised somewhat his level of moral development. Anderson and May paint a picture of Joe McCarthy changing from a shy, hardworking person to a gregarious, backslapping one as he moved onto a broader personal stage. Perhaps a parallel development in the moral sphere now gave him the raw materials he needed to attain the stage Kohlberg calls "morality of cooperation"—where personal relationships induce one to behave properly for the sake of getting along with others. Personal relationships may have become so central to McCarthy's life at this point that his behavior became relatively more socialized, and the heavy hand of his father or of other outside forces was not needed to keep his actions in check. McCarthy's need to be liked, his need for approval and affection may have fostered a morality that accorded well with the emerging new personality Anderson and May describe. Still, the final stage of moral development—to moral guidance through self-accepted principles of conscience—may well have been beyond McCarthy's reach, perhaps forever.

Of course, if Anderson and May are wrong, and O'Brien, Reeves, and Oshinsky are right, the foregoing analysis would have to be discarded, or at least greatly modified. One would turn away from the portrait of an unhappy childhood, and focus instead upon the apolitical nature of McCarthy's world. Whether McCarthy's relationship with his family and with his peers were good or bad, there is little doubt that he came to maturity without a stable and integrated vision of the political world. At Marquette, in his midtwenties, "he neither discussed—nor comprehended—the isms that were stalking the world during the 1930s."[37] Moreover, it seems quite clear that McCarthy's interest in politics, when it did develop, was in the nature of a pure career choice. There was, therefore, no moral or ideological content ever connected with McCarthy's decision to enter politics, except what was needed to make a political candidacy plausible.

When one compares McCarthy in this respect to an archetypical political man, such as James David Barber's active-negative, the differences are striking. Woodrow Wilson, for example, was a deeply religious man who genuinely believed that God had ordered the universe and that all Wilson did was merely part of God's scheme and intended to serve God's purposes. From an early age, he was interested in constitutions and governments, and the pervasiveness of moral and religious teachings (Wilson's father was a Presbyterian minister) became an integral part of his thinking, including his vision of the political world and its purposes. For McCarthy, although he was apparently a deeply observant Roman Catholic in some ways, there simply was no such background of deep moral belief connected to the world of politics. Thus, a fusion of the two could never occur, and by the time McCarthy discovered the political arena, it was a world devoid of any moral purpose or content.

Working with the hypothesis of a McCarthy fixated at a premoral level of development in the realm of politics, it becomes considerably easier to understand how he could behave as outrageously as he did and yet feel no moral twinges or any sense of guilt. Without any inner sense that what he was doing was wrong, McCarthy was able to avoid most of the intrapsychic conflict endemic to the active-negative type. McCarthy had very little need to rationalize his behavior in terms of the public interest, following this line of reasoning, because he saw nothing very wrong with playing out his private motives in the public arena. What McCarthy did was neither right nor wrong; it was simply what he needed and wanted to do. So long as that was his view of the matter, guilt, morality and justification remained completely alien to his mode of thought.

Indeed, evidence of such compartmentalization could be found as early as McCarthy's legal career in Waupaca.

The portrait of McCarthy as someone who had little respect for community values crops up time and again. On occasion, when it suited his purpose or when he felt comfortable in the surroundings, he could behave with proper deference to established tradition and authority. But more often he played the opposite role—the lawless, unsocialized fellow who elbows his way to the center by overwhelming his rule-bound neighbor.[38]

McCarthy was a man "who will break all the rules because for him there are none."[39]

Having come to an awareness of politics relatively late in life, McCarthy never had implanted within him any notion that politics existed for any purpose beyond himself, or that some social betterment was supposed to be the fruit of one's activity in that sphere. Indeed, given the powerful needs that drove McCarthy, it is not at all surprising that he would develop a world view that would allow him the greatest opportunity to satisfy those needs. To see politics as pure stage or arena, available for the playing out of whatever needs or desires impelled him to act, was extremely advantageous from the point of view of McCarthy's psychic economy. Indeed so liberated from such conceptions of politics was McCarthy that, not only did he feel no need to accomplish anything substantive through politics, he did not even feel a need to pretend to be accomplishing anything.

Richard Rovere has suggested that McCarthy was "morally indecent,"[40] but this was true only in the political arena (or perhaps more broadly, in the career arena). In private relationships, McCarthy's desire to be liked and approved of made him a remarkably decent individual, as many contemporary observers freely admitted. Reporters who detested his politics found themselves unable to resist his personal charm. People he treated brutally in public hearings were shocked when McCarthy later offered them private help. Senators attacked vitriolically on the floor of the Senate could not believe it when McCarthy then wanted to be friendly in the cloakroom or cafeteria.

For McCarthy, it was the *political* world that was a jungle—a realm governed by no real rules or norms, a place where every man had to fend for himself in order to attain his goals. And to the extent that the political world was a jungle (or a stage or an arena), it was merely and exclusively a place to satisfy one's private needs. Viewing it from the perspective of Lasswell's formulation, one might say that McCarthy represented the case of a politician displacing his private motives onto public objects, but *without* any need at all to rationalize that displacement in terms of the public interest. Thus the *nature* of the displacement *(d)* made any rationalization *(r)* unnecessary. For McCarthy, the nature of the public arena itself obviated any necessity for justifying his behavior.

Such a belief system as McCarthy's—in which so central a part of his life as the basis for his political activity was sharply cut off from the rest of his thought—could reasonably be expected to produce a schizophrenic personal style. One would predict from such a formulation that a sharp discontinuity would exist between McCarthy's private life and his public, political life. It is no surprise, therefore, to find that numerous observers of McCarthy's career have focused quite sharply upon this precise point, suggesting that McCarthy onstage and McCarthy offstage were two remarkably different people. For McCarthy, what occurred on the public stage bore little relation to his private feelings and relationships. He did not feel himself to be engaged in a life-or-death struggle with an immoral, threatening foe, but rather, merely engaged in an exciting game, the rules of which appeared to him to demand noise and furor in order to gain attention. If that was the nature of the game, then McCarthy was quite willing to play it, but there was certainly no need to pretend it was not a game, or to try to rationalize his behavior to others, who were, presumably, also part of the game. Even for the public, for whom some pretense was perhaps necessary, McCarthy rarely clothed himself in moral righteousness. Rather, he would "immerse himself in the evil around him," and "with sure instinct, he deliberately cultivated the role in which he realized he had been cast—uncouth hero or villain of villains."[41] McCarthy liked to boast "of how he had been instructed by some old North Woods scamp named Indian Charlie to go straight for an adversary's groin whenever he was in serious trouble."[42] The famous anecdote about skunk hunting (quoted in Chapter 2) falls into the same category.

McCarthy's image of politics permitted him a division of the world that would have generated enormous psychological strains for someone with a more integrated world view and a more highly developed sense of morality. Indeed, Barber's active-negative is virtually defined by the conflict he feels between his need for advancement and his need to believe in his own morality. For McCarthy, however, the ability to maintain a strict separation between his private and his public worlds made the issue of morality an irrelevant one. For him, there was no necessary correlation between private and public morality.

In his private life, McCarthy wanted to get along with others and to be liked. But this, he had discovered in his early adulthood, seemed to require winning others' attention. At Manawa, he had slapped backs and told jokes; at Marquette he had boxed and mimicked teachers. Now in the early 1950s, calling people Communists seemed to win the attention of the media, the Washington community, and the public. If there was a payoff for such behavior, McCarthy would certainly engage in it, but this did not mean he actually had to believe in what he was doing. And certainly, by most accounts, McCarthy seems never to have invested much emotional capital in his Communist hunting, beyond that needed to win attention. Thus, the separation, or compartmentalization of private and public stages allowed McCarthy to act easily and without doubts so as to satisfy his basic needs. In the case of Joe McCarthy, one sees therefore the power generated by the reinforcing interaction of needs and political belief system. For more than four years, that combination proved nigh unstoppable.

## Notes

1. Greenstein, *Personality and Politics,* p. 67.
2. Ibid.
3. The major pioneering studies of political socialization include Herbert H. Hyman, *Political Socialization* (New York: Free Press, 1959); David Easton, *Children in the Political System* (New York: McGraw-Hill, 1969); and Kenneth Langton, *Political Socialization* (New York: Oxford University Press, 1969). A good recent statement is Dawson et al., *Political Socialization.*
4. Connell, *Child's Construction of Politics.*
5. Ibid., p. 1.
6. Ibid.
7. Ibid., p. 47. See also Richard M. Merelman, "The Development of Policy Thinking in Adolescence," *American Political Science Review* 65 (December 1971): 1033–47.

8. The ideas outlined here are scattered in numerous writings of Jean Piaget, including *The Construction of Reality in the Child* (New York: Basic Books, 1954); and *The Child's Conception of the World* (London: Routledge and Kegan Paul, 1951). A good summary can be found in J. H. Flavell, *The Developmental Psychology of Jean Piaget* (Princeton: Van Nostrand, 1963).

9. This idea and the analysis that follows are derived chiefly from Connell, *Child's Construction of Politics.*

10. Converse, "Belief Systems." A critique of Converse's description of mass belief systems can be found in W. Lance Bennett, *The Political Mind and the Political Environment* (Lexington, Mass.: Lexington Books, 1975).

11. Lasswell, *Psychopathology and Politics,* p. 262.

12. Ibid., p. 126.

13. See for example, Edward C. Banfield and James Q. Wilson, *City Politics* (New York: Vintage Books, 1963), pp. 329–33, for the distinction between the "public-regarding" and "private-regarding" ethos. See also Arnold Rogow and Harold Lasswell, *Power, Corruption and Rectitude* (Englewood Cliffs, N.J.: Prentice-Hall, 1963), for the distinction between "game" and "gain" politicians.

14. O'Brien, *McCarthyism in Wisconsin,* p. 19.

15. Reeves, *Life and Times,* p. 18.

16. See Robert P. Smith, *Tiger in the Senate* (Garden City, N.Y.: Doubleday, 1962), pp. 34–38, for an account of the impact of Robert La Follette upon Wayne Morse.

17. O'Brien, *McCarthyism in Wisconsin,* p. 18.

18. Griffith, *Politics of Fear,* p. 6. When McCarthy announced for the Senate as a Republican, most Republicans were highly suspicious, regarding him as a New Dealer.

19. Converse, "Belief Systems," p. 207.

20. Robert Lane, *Political Ideology* (New York: Free Press, 1962), p. 15. See also idem., *Political Thinking and Consciousness* (Chicago: Markham, 1969); and idem, *Political Man* (New York: Free Press, 1972).

21. Merelman, "Development of Political Ideology," p. 753.

22. Ibid., p. 757.

23. Piaget, *Moral Judgment of the Child;* Lawerence Kohlberg, "Stage and Sequence: The Cognitive-Developmental Approach to Socialization," in *Handbook of Socialization Theory and Research,* ed. David A. Goslin (Chicago: Rand-McNally, 1969), pp. 347–480. See also idem, "Moral Development," *International Encyclopedia of the Social Sciences,* vol. 10 (New York: Macmillan and Free Press, 1968), pp. 483–94.

24. Kohlberg, "Moral Development," p. 490.

25. This summary is based upon Piaget, *Moral Judgment of the Child.*

26. Kohlberg, "Moral Development," p. 490.

27. Merelman, "Development of Political Ideology," p. 756.

28. Kohlberg, "Moral Development," p. 488.

29. Merelman, "Development of Political Ideology," p. 758.

30. The main proponents of this theory include Robert R. Sears, "Identification as a Form of Behavioral Development," in *The Concept of Development,* ed. Dale B. Harris (Minneapolis: University of Minnesota Press, 1957), pp. 149–62; and John Whiting and Irwin L. Child, *Child Training and Personality* (New Haven: Yale University Press, 1953).

31. Merelman, "Development of Political Ideology," pp. 759–60.

32. Ibid., p. 765.

33. Kohlberg, "Moral Development," p. 492.

34. Ibid.

35. An anonymous Waupaca attorney, quoted in Oshinsky, *Conspiracy So Immense,* p. 16.

36. Merelman, "Development of Political Ideology," p. 768.

37. Reeves, *Life and Times,* p. 18.

38. Oshinsky, *Conspiracy So Immense,* p. 16.

39. Thomas, *When Even Angels Wept,* p. 1.

40. Rovere, *Senator Joe McCarthy,* p. 73.

41. Rogin, *Intellectuals and McCarthy,* p. 229.

42. Rovere, *Senator Joe McCarthy,* p. 49.

# 6
## McCarthy and the 1950s

### The Mystery of McCarthy

The main mystery of Joseph McCarthy, particularly for those too young to remember him in action, is how he managed to succeed for as long as he did. There is, after all, an almost surreal quality to the descriptions of McCarthy at work, making it all too easy to write off the period as one in which America simply went temporarily mad.

> For McCarthyism was, among other things, but perhaps foremost among them, a headlong flight from reality. It elevated the ridiculous and ridiculed the important. It outraged common sense and held common sense to be outrageous. . . . It made sages of screwballs and accused wise men of being fools.[1]

Yet to the extent that one can begin to fathom, even in part, this mystery of McCarthy's success, there is a second mystery. How did McCarthy tumble so quickly and so finally from the heights he had attained? How could the political style that had forced two American presidents to keep his potential impact always in mind bring McCarthy to such complete powerlessness after 1954? In this chapter, I shall review some of the previous answers to these questions, and then try to answer these same questions in terms of the analysis that has preceded.

As noted in Chapter 1, for the "pluralists" there was not much of a mystery about McCarthy's success. The average American did not adhere very strongly to the tenets of democratic thought (except as vague generalities), and given an atmosphere of increased international tensions[2] or domestic status anxieties,[3] he might well respond favorably to the demagogic appeals of someone offering simple solutions to complicated problems. Mass politics was irrational politics, and McCarthy's success could thus be viewed as rooted in another of the periodic outbreaks in America of mass political hysteria and vigilantism. The wild, hysterical tone of McCarthyism represented no more than a clever pandering to the neuroses of the American people, and McCarthy himself was nothing more than a reflection of the desires of the aroused masses. Indeed, for the pluralists, McCarthyism was above all an attack by the masses upon the establishment—the intellectual and political elites of the nation.

And why did McCarthyism come to an end? As tensions and anxieties abated in the mid-1950s, the pluralists explained, the political elites were able to take advantage of the masses' lapsing into their normal quiescence and bring McCarthy to heel. When the American people tired of McCarthy and began to turn against him in the wake of his ugly performance at the Army-McCarthy hearings, the Senate finally had the opportunity to end the Wisconsin senator's reign of terror by moving to censure him. Thus were democratic values reaffirmed—not by the masses' rising up on behalf of those values, but by the elites' functioning through their established institutions to cut down such threats. In sum, "for the pluralists, the concept of mass politics captures both the flavor of McCarthy's appeals and the essence of his threat to American institutions."[4]

Yet as has already been indicated in Chapter 1, most of the empirical evidence regarding McCarthyism points against conceiving of it primarily as a mass phenomenon. One simple measure, the Gallup Poll, for example, shows that "favorable" ratings of McCarthy outweighed "unfavorable" ones in only three of eleven surveys reported, and that the favorable rating reached 50 percent only once. Indeed, the result for August 1951—a year and a half after McCarthy began his crusade and at a time when he was being given credit for enormous power with the American electorate—showed 15 percent of the American people favorable to McCarthy, 22 percent unfavorable, and 63 percent with no opinion.[5]

Moreover, as one looked more closely at the nature of McCarthy's supporters, critics of the pluralists argued, it became clear that, rather than having their roots in the populist tradition, these supporters were very much in the conservative Republican mold. Those supporters who were not conservative Republicans could often be best understood, not as supporters of McCarthy and McCarthyism per se, but as anti-Communists who knew little about McCarthy beyond his identification with the anti-Communist cause. For many of these people, Communism was indeed more of a foreign policy issue than a domestic one.[6] Thus, even among those who did have a favorable view of McCarthy, support was hardly unqualified. As Nelson Polsby put it in 1960:

> The essential aimlessness of McCarthy's appeal could be deduced, for example, from the fact that McCarthy support seems to have been highly diffused and multidimensional, rather than effectively mobilized and focused on concrete political goals.[7]

Polsby's analysis pointed away from the view of McCarthyism as a mass phenomenon and toward what he termed a "political interpretation"—that

McCarthyism was rooted in traditional partisan politics rather than in some anomic mass movement outside the American mainstream. As pursued by Michael Rogin, this analysis was extended to argue that McCarthy was to be viewed primarily as an instrument wielded by one section of America's political elite against the other. The Republican party, frustrated by twenty years of the New Deal and the Fair Deal, was willing to do virtually anything to return to power. McCarthy's charges seemed the perfect vehicle for such a return, and the Republicans succumbed easily to the temptation laid before them. Even Robert Taft—"Mr. Republican" and normally a paragon of integrity—who had at first complained privately about McCarthy's "perfectly reckless performance" was all too quickly willing to declare publicly that McCarthy should "keep talking and if one case doesn't work out, he should proceed with another one."[8] In sum, McCarthy really had no "cohesive, organized popular following," and "in so far as McCarthy challenged political decisions, political individuals, and the political fabric, he was sustained not by a revolt of the masses so much as by the actions and inactions of various elites."[9]

A variant of this view that elites were responsible for McCarthyism can be found in the work of those revisionist students of the cold war who see the origins of McCarthyism less in Republican actions than in the decisions of the Truman administration and the Democrats to pursue a cold war against the Soviet Union and to establish loyalty programs for federal employees. "Given the rhetoric of the Truman Administration," concludes Athan Theoharis, for example, "the McCarthyite attack was neither irrational nor aberrational so much as the logical extension of Administration policies and assumptions. On February 9, 1950, at Wheeling, West Virginia, the crows simply began coming home to roost."[10] Having legitimatized the notion of an internal Communist threat, the Democrats should hardly have been surprised when the Republicans decided to make full use of the weapon they had so conveniently been handed.

A somewhat milder, although ultimately still critical, assessment of the responsibility of President Truman for the rise of McCarthyism can be found in the work of Richard Freeland.[11] He suggests that the Truman administration's decision in 1947 to seek approval of the Marshall Plan by placing it in the context of the struggle against Communism generated fears in an American public that had till then been relatively unworried about the Soviet Union. McCarthyism might therefore be most properly viewed, this argument runs, as an unintended side effect of a political strategy chosen by the Democrats to secure passage of a program deemed vital to American security interests in Europe.

Defenders of the Truman administration and the Democrats have, of course, also had their say. Alan Harper argues for the validity of the traditional view that Stalin began the cold war and that there was at least some basis for the fear of internal Communist subversion.[12] From this perspective, President Truman is seen as involved in a delicate balancing act between the demands of America's civil liberties tradition and the need for national security. Richard Fried makes the case that the revisionists have failed to take sufficiently into account the fact that "the 'red' issue enjoyed an independent growth pattern of its own," and that consequently, though "the Democrats had made many errors . . . at most stages their prospects for success had been sharply limited by the fact that McCarthy's power arose from long-term political trends over which they had only slight control."[13] Robert Griffith, somewhat more critical of the Democrats than either Harper or Fried, although not willing to place direct blame on them for the creation of McCarthyism, suggests that the main sin of the Democrats (and for that matter, the moderate Republicans) was one of omission rather than commission. As Griffith puts it, "Perhaps this was the real key to McCarthy's continued power—not the ranting of demagogues, but the fear and irresolution of honorable men."[14]

All of the views so far described—of McCarthyism as the creation of the American people, as a weapon wielded by conservative Republican politicians, and as a technique legitimatized (directly or indirectly) or at least acquiesced in by the Democrats—are of course views that emphasize the environment within which McCarthyism developed. It would be foolish to attempt to deny the force of environmental variables in contributing first to McCarthy's success and then to his political demise.

But one comes back again to the nature of McCarthyism, as distinguished from other forms of American anti-Communism. Anti-Communism can certainly be seen as the kind of weapon a frustrated political elite might use (even use unfairly) against another political elite in power. But elite conflict in America is not normally anything so wild or chaotic or senseless as McCarthyism was. What, after all, is one to make of the charge that General George C. Marshall, one of the most respected men in the country, was part of a "conspiracy and an infamy so black as to dwarf any previous such venture in the history of man."[15] Is this simply part of the hyperbole traditional in American political life?

How does one come to grips with the famous Senate speech of 20 February 1950 in which McCarthy attempted to defend the charges made in his Wheeling speech eleven days earlier? Going through his list of "those I consider to be Communists in the State Department," McCarthy reached Case 72, notable according to McCarthy,

> in that it is the direct opposite of the cases I have been reading. . . . I do not confuse this man as being a Communist. This individual was very highly recommended by several witnesses as a high type of man, a Democratic American who . . . opposed Communism.[16]

Also, the man had never worked for the State Department.

Is it typical of elite conflict in America that when a member of this elite is approached by reporters looking for a story, he mulls the matter over for a few moments and then reaches into his pocket where he keeps a supply of blank subpoenas and begins to make one out for a former president of the United States?

> "You're not serious, Joe; you can't be," one of the reporters said. "The hell I'm not serious," McCarthy said. "I'll have this filled out in a second." "What are you going to subpoena him for?" he was asked. McCarthy tapped his big skull with his fountain pen. "Oh, I'm calling him to testify about Harry Dexter White, that's what I'm calling him for." [17]

Clearly, in these examples, there is something at work that transcends purely environmental explanations. While environmental factors are, of course, necessary to an understanding of McCarthyism, that phenomenon cannot be understood *solely* in such terms. If it is true that the environment made McCarthyism possible, it is equally true that Joseph McCarthy made McCarthyism necessary. Without an environment supportive of his activities, McCarthyism would not have flourished. But without McCarthy, there would have been no McCarthyism, as that term is known.

Anti-Communism had been a strand in America's political thought and behavior for over thirty years when McCarthy came to power; it continued after McCarthy's death. Certainly it is true that elements of McCarthyism can be found in anti-Communism pre- and post-McCarthy, but on the whole, there was something special about the character of McCarthy's own crusade that was not duplicated in the efforts of Martin Dies, J. Parnell Thomas, Richard Nixon, William Jenner, or Francis Walter. If the search for subversives resumes a central place in American politics in the future, it is highly unlikely that it will take a McCarthyite form, with all that is implied by that term. The randomness of targets, the haphazard development of so-called evidence, and the lack of concern for following through made McCarthyism a special business indeed. It is that special quality that can only be understood by a careful analysis of Joseph McCarthy's political style—its sources, its nature, and its consequences.

Traditionally, social science has had something of a bias against explanation in terms of individuals and in favor of theories rooted in broad, environmental factors. One writer on McCarthyism has been praised, for example, because

> his analysis has the advantage of removing McCarthy from the lime-light—a fortuitous development, it would appear—since the Wisconsin

Republican's bombast and primitive style mesmerized liberal historians
as they did liberal politicians during the early 1950's.[18]

Yet the truth is that, almost from the beginning, McCarthy's own role in
McCarthyism was played down in favor of broader explanations. After
Jack Anderson and Ronald May's biography was published in 1952, and
Reinhard Luthin devoted a chapter to McCarthy in his book on American
demagogues, emphasis shifted very quickly to the exogenous factors at
work. Daniel Bell's *New American Right,* published in 1955, moved
rapidly to place McCarthyism in historical, sociological, and psychological perspective. While studies since then have not exactly neglected Mc-
Carthy himself, he has, to a considerable extent, been treated as a given,
with most actual analysis centering around the question of what elements
of American society and politics were responsible for his success.

In light of this trend, perhaps it is not unfair to suggest that what is
needed is a theory of McCarthyism that will compensate for what has
become an excessive reliance upon broad, systemic factors for an explanation of that phenomenon. If history is about human beings, then Mc-
Carthyism, like any historical episode, necessarily represents an
interaction of personal and environmental factors, and McCarthy's success can therefore only be understood in terms of both. While it certainly
can be said that McCarthyism flourished and then faded because the
American political environment of the early 1950s permitted and even
encouraged it, and then came to oppose and condemn it, it must also be
admitted that McCarthyism rose and fell because of the kind of man
McCarthy was.

Thus, one would do well to heed the warning of Harold Lasswell that

> when the tumultuous life of society is flayed into precedents and tanned
> into principles, the resulting abstractions suffer a strange fate. They are
> grouped and regrouped until the resulting mosaic may constitute a
> logical and aesthetic whole which has long ceased to bear any valid
> relation to the original reality. Concepts are constantly in danger of
> losing their reference to definite events.[19]

For Lasswell, it was the role of political biography to furnish a "vivid
corrective" to the overemphasis laid upon the study of structures and
systems. "Political science without biography is a form of taxidermy,"[20]
he concluded.

Thus, I turn to Joseph McCarthy's style, for it is that style which
constitutes the missing link between what the pluralists have viewed as the
mass style exemplified in McCarthyism, and what their critics have seen
as more fundamentally a matter of elite conflict. In the previous two
chapters, I probed the sources of McCarthy's style, and was able to

suggest that his motivational system and his cognitive and moral development fostered an impulsive style that came to characterize McCarthy's behavior in the political arena. In this chapter, I will carry the analysis forward in order to explain the consequences of that style for American politics in the 1950s. Why and how did the impulsive style carry McCarthy to great heights of power in the period from 1950 to 1954, and then cast him down in 1954, never to rise again?

### The Impulsive Type in Politics

The impulsive style, as noted earlier, allows for great tactical flexibility. In the short run, the impulsive style may prove highly adaptive in an environment "where readiness to quick action or expression and/or a facility for competence of a sort that may be developed in pursuit of immediate and egocentric interests can be useful."[21] Studies of the impulsive type conducted by David Kipnis showed, for example, that while this type was likely to be exploitive of others and less likely than others to be inhibited in his behavior by conventional social values, shame and anxiety, or social influence, these traits were not always maladaptive. Indeed, in some contexts, these traits were likely to be of value to the possessor, and would be socially approved.[22] Thus, the impulsive type cannot be viewed simply as a wild man on the loose. Depending upon circumstances, the impulsive may succeed or fail.

The impulsive type has one powerful advantage in the day-to-day world of politics. Not bound to any set of values or ideals beyond the satisfaction of his own self-interest, the impulsive type is able to operate with great efficiency. Unburdened by the normal demands of conscience, beliefs, or ideology, the impulsive type has available to him enormous energies for use in the outside world. Virtually no psychic energy needs to be employed in the resolution of inner conflicts, for there are no doubts or guilt feelings to engender such conflicts. Unlike the active-negative type described by James Barber, for example, the impulsive does not find himself engaged in a perpetual, draining inner struggle to help him rationalize his actions to himself in terms of some moral principle.

Thus, the impulsive type can be seen as embodying, almost to the $n$th degree, the public's stereotypical conception of the politician as one who will say or do anything in order to be elected. Whatever needs to be said or done in order to satisfy his needs, the impulsive is able to say or do with virtually no thought given to social proprieties or broader consequences. If the only way to assure one's daily quota of media coverage and public notoriety is, for example, to supply a Communist a day, the impulsive can cast about almost at random for one to offer up. Without the "albatrosses" of ideology or conscience, the impulsive can run wild, flitting from charge to charge, never bogged down by matters so petty as evidence or ethics.

What was unique, then, about Joe McCarthy's political style was his lack of anchoring principles and beliefs. For him, the political world was born anew every day. What had happened yesterday bore no necessary connection to what would happen today. And what was done today was not necessarily related to what would happen tomorrow. It all depended upon what struck a responsive chord with the press and the public, and for just how long that response could be counted upon. If the press and the public seemed to be losing interest in a particular charge, then McCarthy was perfectly content to move on to something a bit more spectacular. That yesterday's supposed Communist in high places was presumably being left behind to pursue his nefarious activities unhindered hardly seemed to matter.

In short-range tactical terms, McCarthy's approach was, of course, highly rational. What was the point, after all, of losing the press and the public in the complexities of any one case when fresh ones were all around, waiting to be exploited for their publicity value and then forgotten? McCarthy's impulsive style, never hampered by conventional notions of right and wrong, never squeamish about harm done to a reputation, never worried about what his colleagues thought, was a perfect one for the unsettled political climate of the early 1950s. "He had learned back in Wisconsin that the penalties for a really audacious mendacity are not as severe as the average politician fears them to be, that, in fact, there may be no penalties at all, but only profit."[23]

Thus was McCarthy unleashed, and a style so reckless and unrestrained could not easily be coped with, given the willingness of elements of the political elite to legitimatize his actions and the "fear and irresolution of honorable men" who would not stand up against him. One has only to look at how the press came to deal with McCarthy in order to understand how his particular style was able to carry him as far as it did.

> Few newspapers could print—because few readers would read—reports of a length sufficient to give the true gamey flavor of the performance. Even if they had wished to do so, it would have been difficult to get the reports, for McCarthy's presentation had been so disorderly, so jumbled and cluttered and loose-ended, that it was beyond the power of most reporters to organize the mess into a story that would convey to the reader anything beyond the suspicion that the reporter was drunk. There was a bedlam quality to McCarthy's speeches that seldom got through to those who never read them.[24]

It seems clear, then, that in the case of McCarthy one is dealing with something out of the ordinary for political elites. To be precise, it would appear to be a manifestation of what Philip Converse has called the "mass belief system"—a state of mind marked by fragmentation and volatility of political ideas. Such a belief system is one in which political ideas and opinions are only minimally related (if at all) to one another, and are subject to great fluctuation over relatively short periods of time. To Converse, such fragmentation and instability was characteristic of the belief systems of the masses, as contrasted to the more ideological, structured modes of political thought associated with political elites. Whether this distinction is a valid one continues to be debated by political scientists.[25] Nonetheless, that this sort of belief system exists in some people does not seem open to serious doubt.

The implication of this is that fragmented, unstable political belief systems can probably be found in considerable numbers in the general population, though the extent and degree of that fragmentation and instability may certainly vary considerably. Although one might not expect people with such belief systems to enter politics, it is possible that at least some do. When one considers, for example, the tendency to view local politics as a matter of nonpartisan (hence nonpolitical) housekeeping, the lack of coherent political beliefs might well be less of a handicap than expected. Given sufficient motive, adequate resources, and the right opportunity, it seems quite likely that some people manifesting the impulsive style seek to enter the political arena every year, and that some succeed.

Why, then, are there not innumerable Joe McCarthys running through our political system? Presumably the answer lies in the conservative tendencies of the American political system and its institutions. America's political parties, for example, have long been viewed as agencies for the screening out of those who are seen as not fitting into the existing political structure. V. O. Key has spoken of party opposition to the rise of primaries in terms of the leadership finding "its choice for nomination defeated in the primary by a banjo player, a demagogue who ought to be in the other party, or some other bizarre person."[26]

Moreover, those who might slip through this net of party screening would normally be rendered harmless by the web of rules, procedures, and customs that govern America's political institutions. A network of institutional norms could be expected to tie down such potential deviants, or at least quickly isolate them from the possibility of assuming power. While there has been considerable debate over the extent to which mavericks are tolerated in a body like the United States Senate, it is certainly true that even mavericks have to function within certain limits, and that passing those limits triggers sanctions.[27]

McCarthy can perhaps thus best be seen as the rare figure demonstrating that the statistical improbability is nonetheless possible. One cannot reasonably guess at the number of impulsives seeking to begin a political career in America in 1939, but given the functioning of the American political system, it is likely that many of them were screened out rather quickly or confined to low-level offices. As time went on, fewer and fewer of those 1939 impulsives were of any political significance. Given a political style that may be highly effective in the short run, but that seems inevitably to fail when put to the long-term test, this would seem to be clear. Nonetheless, one man was able to defy the odds against the impulsive style and rise to the office of United States senator. Helped no doubt by the unusually weak party system that was a legacy of Wisconsin's Progressive heritage, McCarthy was able to get much further than the impulsive type has any right to expect, and in 1947, he took his seat in the Senate.

At this point, one would certainly have been entitled to assume that McCarthy had reached his apogee. Indeed, the next two years seemed clear proof of this, as McCarthy stumbled about with no clear sense of direction, leading many to believe that he would not be reelected in 1952. Then suddenly in February 1950, with his famous speech at Wheeling, West Virginia, McCarthy found his issue. The Communist issue had already worked for him three months earlier in the arena of Wisconsin politics, and now McCarthy was ready to take the show on the road before the American people.[28] For various reasons already described, the issue assumed a life of its own, and McCarthy was precisely the right man in the right spot at the right moment. The impulsive style meshed almost perfectly with the dynamics of American politics—for just about four years.

Of course, it was all bound to end, and in the same way that the concept of the impulsive style helps to explain the reasons for Joe McCarthy's success, it helps to explain the reasons for his ultimate failure. For although changes in the political environment certainly occurred after the Eisenhower administration took over, a more adaptive political style might well have enabled McCarthy to make the adjustments necessary for continued success in the changed political atmosphere. But, as was noted, the impulsive style is generally adaptive only in the short run. In the long term, the impulsive seems doomed to blunder, for he cannot easily control his inner needs. There may be superb competence demonstrated in the tactical realm, where the impulsive shows a real talent for quick adjustments. Nonetheless, there is an underlying inflexibility that sooner or later manifests itself. Though the impulsive may very skillfully go after what he wants, he cannot control what he wants, or the intensity with which he wants it. Kipnis, in his study of impulsives, suggests that, as compared to the average person, they are "in greater need of excitement and social stimulation."[29] McCarthy needed his publicity and his sense of public acclaim, and so long as his tactics brought him the glory he sought, all was well. But the coming to power of the Republicans in 1953 threatened to interfere with the satisfaction of that need.

McCarthy's need for attention did not disappear with the accession of Dwight Eisenhower to the presidency. Initially, he showed some willingness to look in other directions for the glory he needed, but the prospects were not promising. After the 1952 election, McCarthy publicly announced that he could now give up hunting subversives, and concentrate instead upon exposing "graft and corruption." The fact that Majority Leader Robert Taft had chosen to make William Jenner of Indiana the new chairman of the Senate Internal Security Committee seemed at first to leave the Wisconsin senator with little choice. Taft, in fact, boasted of how "he had engineered a brilliant coup by bottling McCarthy up in Government Operations, where he would spend his days studying reports from the General Accounting Office."[30]

It did not take McCarthy very long to understand where things were headed, and very quickly he began maneuvering for a role in the investigation of domestic Communism for his committee's Permanent Subcommittee on Investigations. McCarthy understood that there simply was nothing like "Communists in goverment" to win him the easy headlines he sought. It was not very long before Roy Cohn had been brought on board as chief counsel for the subcommittee, and soon McCarthy was on the warpath once more. Though now under Republican direction, the State Department, the Voice of America, and America's overseas libraries were made targets of investigation. During the summer of 1953, a one-day hearing was held regarding a "plot" to assassinate McCarthy, and plans were announced to investigate the Atomic Energy Commission, the Central Intelligence Agency, and the military.[31]

In late 1953, McCarthy met with Vice President Richard Nixon and Deputy Attorney General William Rogers in Miami, giving them the impression that he was now prepared to back off from his confrontation with the Eisenhower administration and move into other areas of investigation. "With his committee's appropriation once again before the Senate, he continued to foster the illusion that he might lay off both the Administration and the Communist issue."[32] Two months later, McCarthy called General Ralph Zwicker before his committee, and the events that culminated in the Army-McCarthy hearings were underway. The end was in sight for Joseph McCarthy.

Clearly, the impulsive style that had made McCarthy so great a success from 1950 to 1954 had its limitations. In some ways, he was like a general whose tactical maneuvers can be stunningly brilliant, but whose taste for blood leads him into wars that simply cannot be won.

In "Political Science and Political Biography," Lewis Edinger in the

1960s suggested that "the test of successful and effective political leadership would seem to be the apparent congruence of the aspiring leader's role perception with those of his counter-players in a relevant role set."[33] One who wishes to lead politically will succeed to the extent that others share, or at least acquiesce in, his view of himself as a leader. "Sometimes such a person is called a great leader," noted Edinger, "sometimes an astute politician, sometimes a demagogue."[34] The lack of congruence between a leader's role perceptions and those of his counter-players can sometimes be concealed for a time by a skillful enough leader, but "in the case of persistent incongruence, the voters will retire a central actor, a revolution overthrow him, his formal subordinates fail to execute his orders."[35] Nonetheless, before such incongruence becomes plain—before it becomes clear to others that their leader has goals in mind rather different from their own—there may be considerable time for those in leadership roles to do as they wish and get what they want. There is, in other words, sufficient slack in the relationship to allow for what has been described as the "opportunist role." Discerned originally in the legislative arena, this type "mainly uses the legislative office or 'plays at' the legislative role while concealing that he is really playing other, essentially non-legislative roles."[36]

Ultimately, however, given a political environment in which it is essentially impossible for both the leader's goals and those of his counter-players to be satisfied, the slack will disappear, and something will have to give. So long as Joe McCarthy's goals and those of his conservative Republican supporters were attuned, it was possible for him to hold sway. After the Eisenhower administration came to power, McCarthy's goals and those of the Republican party moved increasingly out of synchronization, and the great impulsive energies that had taken him to the heights of power and influence now impelled him just as strongly toward political destruction.

Had McCarthy been able to satisfy his need for acclaim and glory by generating front-page stories with his studies of General Accounting Office reports, there would have been no conflict between him and the Eisenhower administration. But the reality of mid-1950s America was that no issue seemed so well suited to generating headlines as the Communist issue—and so, the Communist issue it had to be. That the time was no longer right for it simply could not be comprehended by McCarthy. Thus, from January 1953, when Eisenhower took office, to December 1954, when the U.S. Senate censured McCarthy, the Wisconsin senator was merely playing out a doomed hand. But then, McCarthy was always a poker player, and no one should have known better than he that in order to win big, one must always be ready to lose big.

## Notes

1. Rovere, *Senator Joe McCarthy,* p. 40.

2. See Samuel Lubell, *The Future of American Politics,* 2d ed. (Garden City, N.Y.: Doubleday, 1956), p. 164; and Talcott Parsons, "Social Strains in America," in *The Radical Right,* ed. Daniel Bell (Garden City, N.Y.: Anchor Books, 1963), pp. 209–11.

3. See Richard Hofstadter, "The Pseudo-Conservative Revolt"; Peter Viereck, "The Revolt against the Elite"; and Seymour Martin Lipset, "The Sources of the 'Radical Right,'" all in *The Radical Right,* ed. Bell.

4. Rogin, *Intellectuals and McCarthy,* p. 217.

5. Ibid., p. 232.

6. Ibid., pp. 232–48.

7. Polsby, "Explanation of McCarthyism," p. 270.

8. Patterson, *Mr. Republican,* p. 446.

9. Rogin, *Intellectuals and McCarthy,* p. 248.

10. Athan Theoharis, "The Politics of Scholarship: Liberals, Anti-Communism, and McCarthyism," in *The Specter: Original Essays on the Cold War and the Origins of McCarthyism,* ed. Robert Griffith and Athan Theoharis (New York: New Viewpoints, 1974).

11. Freeland, *Truman Doctrine.*

12. Harper, *Politics of Loyalty.*

13. Fried, *Men Against McCarthy.*

14. Griffith, *Politics of Fear,* p. 151.

15. Booth Mooney, *The Politicians* (Philadelphia: Lippincott, 1970), p. 110.

16. Rovere, *Senator Joe McCarthy,* pp. 132–33.

17. Ibid., p. 165.

18. Geoffrey S. Smith, "'Harry, We Hardly Know You': Revisionism, Politics and Diplomacy, 1945–1954," *American Political Science Review* 70 (June 1976): 575.

19. Lasswell, *Psychopathology and Politics,* p. 1.

20. Ibid.

21. Shapiro, *Neurotic Styles,* p. 147.

22. David Kipnis, *Character Structure and Impulsiveness* (New York: Academic Press, 1971), pp. 114–17.

23. Rovere, *Senator Joe McCarthy,* p. 140.

24. Ibid., p. 137.

25. Converse, "Belief Systems," pp. 206–61. Converse's views about mass belief systems are disputed in Bennett, *Political Mind and Environment.*

26. V. O. Key, Jr., *Politics, Parties and Pressure Groups,* 5th ed. (New York: Thomas Y. Crowell, 1964), p. 386.

27. The nature of Senate norms relating to mavericks is debated in Donald R. Matthews, *U.S. Senators and Their World* (Chapel Hill: University of North Carolina Press, 1960); Ralph K. Huitt, "The Outsider in the Senate: An Alternative Role," *American Political Science Review* 55 (September 1961): 566–75; and Donald R. Matthews, "Can the Outsider's Role Be Legitimate?" *American Political Science Review* 55 (December 1961): 882–83.

28. Michael O'Brien, "McCarthy and McCarthyism: The Cedric Parker Case, November 1949," in Griffith and Theoharis, *The Specter,* pp. 224–38.

29. Kipnis, *Character Structure,* p. 113.

30. Rovere, *Senator Joe McCarthy,* p. 188.

31. Griffith, *Politics of Fear,* p. 216.

32. Ibid., p. 220.

33. Lewis Edinger, "Political Science and Political Biography," in *Political Leadership: Readings for an Emerging Field,* ed. Glenn Paige (New York: Free Press, 1972), p. 222.

34. Ibid.

35. Ibid., p. 223.

36. John C. Wahlke, Heinz Eulau, William Buchanan, and LeRoy C. Ferguson, *The Legislative System* (New York: Wiley, 1962), p. 249.

# 7

## Conclusions: Demagoguery in American Politics

A character as intriguing as Joseph McCarthy and a time as traumatic as the McCarthy era inevitably force one to ask whether there are larger lessons to be learned from studying them. At least two broad questions immediately suggest themselves in this respect: (1) What can be learned from McCarthy's life about the nature of political leadership in the United States? and (2) Is a revival of McCarthyism in America possible?

Beginning with the first question, it may be useful to consider the concept of the *demagogue* in relation to McCarthy. That word has frequently been used in trying to place McCarthy in some broader context and thereby coming to understand McCarthyism in historical perspective. Perhaps, however, this usual procedure can be reversed, and McCarthy can be used to shed more light on the meaning of the term *demagogue*. Such an approach may then permit some general comments about the place of this style of political leadership in American life.

The concept of demagoguery has not been a very fruitful one for political science. It appears only once, for example, in the *Handbook of Political Science*.[1] The reason for this paucity seems fairly clear—the normative connotations of the term have made it a relatively unattractive concept for the behavioral sciences. A high degree of subjectivity is inevitably involved in attempts to use the term, for one man's demagogue may well be another's statesman. As the authors of one of the few empirically based works on demagoguery put it: "To say the least, operationalizing the concept *demagoguery* is no simple task."[2] Nonetheless, although it might prove difficult in practice to secure agreement as to who is or is not a demagogue, this ought not to prevent attempts to refine the definition and pursue some of the implications flowing from such a definition. What is interesting, therefore, is the absence of much intensive effort aimed at working out some of the complexities involved in making sense of demagoguery as a political phenomenon.

One can begin by looking at two or three major definitions developed over the years. The *Oxford English Dictionary* suggests as a second definition (the first harking back to the original Greek meaning of "a leader of the people"):

> In bad sense: A leader of a popular faction or of the mob; a political agitator who appeals to the passions and prejudices of the mob in order to obtain power or further his own interests; an unprincipled or factious popular orator.[3]

The *American Political Dictionary* proposes:

> An unscrupulous politician who seeks to win and hold office through emotional appeals to mass prejudices and passions. Half-truths, outright lies, and various means of card-stacking may be used in attempts to dupe the voters. Typically a demagogue may try to win support from one group by blaming another for its misfortunes.[4]

William Safire in *The New Language of Politics* is content to define a demagogue as

> one who appeals to greed, fear, and hatred; an attack word implying a spellbinding orator, careless with facts and a danger to rational decisions.[5]

Finally, David Bennett in *Demagogues in the Depression* notes:

> Many men and movements appeared . . . offering to solve the pressing and perplexing problem of privation in the midst of plenty in affluent America. These men were true demagogues. Stirring up the prejudices and passions of the population by tricks of rhetoric and sensational charges, by specious arguments, catchwords and cajolery, the demagogue tried to play on discontents and to intensify the original irrational elements within them. By so doing, he sought to seduce his followers into an emotional attachment to his person that would effectively block any group awareness of either the real sources of unhappiness or the real means of solution.[6]

There are sufficient areas of similarity among these definitions that it quickly becomes possible to pull out two or three major strands as constituting the main fabric of demagoguery. First, there is the question of means. Demagogues employ means that play upon the emotions, prejudices, and irrationalities of the public. Second, there is the question of ends. Demagogues prevent people from seeking genuine solutions to their problems by proposing simple answers that are more immediately attractive. Third, there is the question of the demagogue's motivation. His motives are usually primarily personal ones, in that his major interest is in his own power and status rather than the good of the people for whom he professes concern.

The three elements of demagoguery outlined above point quite clearly to the problems involved in making effective use of the concept. If one chooses to focus, for example, on the element of the means employed by a demagogue, problems arise very quickly. Virtually all political leaders rely upon emotional appeals to some extent in seeking to win and hold office, and in attempting to secure the policies they desire. Presumably the intensity and the frequency of such appeals are relevant to the definition, but these are obviously aspects difficult to measure accurately. Moreover, there are various kinds of emotions to which political leaders can appeal. Most definitions of *demagoguery* associate demagogues with appeals to such unhealthy or base emotions as hatred, greed, prejudice, or anger. Although appeals to love, brotherhood, or selflessness might also be viewed as appeals to emotion, not many would view the purveyors of such sentiments as demagogic.

In terms of ends, demagogues are frequently seen as calling for policies that represent simple answers to complicated problems. In Mason and Jaros's "Alienation and Support for Demagogues," for example, their simulation of a demagogic candidate consists of his statement that

> Communists have already taken over 90% of the government; taking up arms may be the only way to get it back. We cannot rest until there is no Communist left on this earth and decency has been restored.[7]

Thus, a demagogue offers solutions that are unrealistic or even dangerous (in that they distract people from the true problems and the true solutions). The advocacy of simple solutions can be seen as fitting together neatly with the demagogue's attempts to arouse intense public feeling through the methods he employs. If one accepts the frequently stated view that the public is relatively limited in its ability to grasp complex and subtle public policy issues, the demagogue's choice of simple solutions becomes a necessity, given the emotional appeals he is likely to be making. It does not seem likely that a demagogue could go far with a highly emotional appeal for some policy proposal incomprehensible to the average citizen.

What is involved then, in terms of both means and ends, in the functioning of the demagogue is the tendency toward *simplification*. Emotional appeals can be immediately and easily grasped, without the effort and costs involved in deciphering and analyzing appeals to rationality. Simple ends are more easily comprehended than complex ones. Thus, one could propose that an ideal-type demagogue would be one who uses appeals to the baser emotions as a way of convincing people to accept simplistic solutions to their problems. At the other end of the spectrum would be the political leader who seeks to move people toward complex (that is, truer) solutions to their problems by appealing chiefly to the public's rationality.

Structuring the definition of demagoguery in this way has the advantage of pointing toward two mixed types generated by the typology based on means and ends. What is one to say about the leader who seeks to move people toward complex ends through primarily emotional appeals, or the leader who strives to move the public toward simplistic ends through appeals to rationality? Serious, substantial political leaders with respectable programs, but of a somewhat unprincipled (some might call it simply realistic) bent could be seen as falling into the first category. Simple-minded (perhaps extremist) political leaders more comfortable with rational persuasion than emotional appeals might constitute the second category. Whether these mixed types ought really to be regarded as demagogues at all is, of course, problematic. It could certainly be argued in the first case that seriousness of purpose and goodness of ends ought to be weighed in the balance against charges of demagoguery arising out of the nature of the leader's appeals. Indeed, one could find many in the 1950s who were willing to express disapproval of Senator McCarthy's methods while insisting that he was basically on the right track. In *McCarthy and His Enemies,* William Buckley and L. Brent Bozell sought to defend McCarthy, at least in part, by claiming Franklin Roosevelt as his spiritual ancestor.[8] Their argument suggested that McCarthy's approach to the public was not much different from FDR's and that to the extent their ends could be viewed as legitimate, their methods were perhaps not so significant.

In the second case—of simplistic ends advocated in a fairly rational way—it would certainly not be out of place to suggest that extremism and demagoguery ought not to be regarded as precise equivalents. In more recent American politics, Barry Goldwater and George McGovern have been regarded by some as extremists, but few would regard these essentially mild-mannered men as exemplars of demagoguery.

Turning finally to the third element of this attempt at a definition—the demagogue's prime concern only for his own power and not for the good of the people he seeks to lead—one must ask how this aspect fits in with the ideal-type demagogue sketched above. Certainly there is an aspect of the term *demagoguery* that suggests telling the people what they want to hear. H. L. Mencken, for example, once spoke of the need in American politics to "flatter and enchant the boobs with blah."[9]

Is the ideal-type demagogue to be seen, therefore, as necessarily insincere in his advocacy of programs, or might he sometimes be a true believer in what he is urging upon the people? Could not a demagogue be a zealous adherent to his cause, as Adolf Hitler certainly was in respect to anti-Semitism? Presumably it would be an odd definition of demagogue that excluded a figure like Hitler. Yet it is certainly true that at least some of those who have been labeled demagogues were cynical, emotionally detached persons who viewed their causes as purely instrumental to their ends. Bennett's study of *Demagogues in the Depression* concludes that there were differences in "basic motivation" between men like William Lemke and Francis Townsend, who spent their lives fighting for causes in which they believed, and men like Gerald L. K. Smith and Father Coughlin who "were always chamaeleonlike . . . in search of a movement that would bring them fame and power."[10]

While it could be argued that demagoguery can be defined and analyzed most objectively purely in behavioral terms, and that inner motivations are largely irrelevant to an understanding of the phenomenon, I shall pursue the view that internal states do matter. Viewing demagoguery purely in terms of the relationship between the leader and the led, without taking into account the attitudes of the leader regarding what he is doing seems shortsighted. If one wishes to ultimately understand not just the consequences, but the causes of demagoguery, and to be able to judge more accurately its prospects for success or failure, one probably needs first to confront directly this definitional question of demagogue as true believer or as opportunist.

What seems to be the case is that either of these inner states can be associated with demagogic behavior, and that therefore such states cannot be used to distinguish demagogues from nondemagogues—that is, they are not part of the basic definition of the concept. Rather, one must distinguish between two types of demagogue—the crusader-demagogue and the opportunist-demagogue. Thus, although inner motivation is not a distinguishing characteristic in terms of defining demagoguery, it nonetheless plays an important role in such matters as likelihood of success.

The crusader-demagogue will bring greater genuine passion to his cause, and to the extent that the public is able to sense genuine feeling, he will either be able to accumulate a greater following or frighten people away. The opportunist-demagogue, on the other hand, is likely to be considerably more flexible in his maneuverings. Indeed, he is likely to be able to jettison causes that no longer appear to be working effectively for him, while the crusader-demagogue will hold onto his cause beyond any useful point. Depending on a variety of external circumstances, one type or the other is likely to prove more successful at particular times and places. In broad terms, one might think of the crusader-demagogue as being initially carried along further by the thrust of great passion, but of the opportunist-demagogue has having greater staying power due to his tactical flexibility as public moods change.

There is, however, one additional factor that must be considered in regard to the opportunist-demagogue. What would be the nature of the psychic strain involved in advocating intensely causes one does not truly believe in? How comfortable would a politician be knowing that he was acting solely from motives of power seeking and ambition? Lasswell's paradigm for the political man presumably included the notion of rationalization in terms of the public interest precisely because he regarded it as unlikely that a person could live with a view of himself as unmotivated by anything except personal ambition.

Every politician presumably does and says some things he does not believe in, in the expectation that these will help him gain and hold power; to this extent, every politician could be said to be something of a demagogue. The great political observer, Frank Kent, devoted a chapter in *The Great Game of Politics* to what he called "Humbuggery in Every Campaign," arguing that

> no man, however genuine, can afford in a fight to give his opponent the tremendous advantage that complete frankness about himself and his views would give. Hence, as a matter of self-preservation, all candidates deceive the voters more or less—some to a large extent and on important issues, others to a small degree and on trivial issues—but they all humbug a little.[11]

In a somewhat different way, the well-known concept of a dichotomy between "Delegate" and "Trustee" as styles of representation also draws attention to the gap between what a politician may believe and what he does.[12] While the Trustee sees himself as responsible for acting on his own judgment, no matter what his constituency may feel, the Delegate sees himself as no more than a recorder of his constituency's views. Thus, the Delegate suppresses his own feelings and views in the interests of maintaining what he regards as the purpose of representative government. (More cynical observers might note that such a view provides an excellent rationalization for doing nothing that might jeopardize one's tenure in office.)

In any event, one can see that a key question for any politician in a system where public opinion matters involves the extent to which he feels justified in compromising himself in order to remain in office or advance to higher office. James Barber's active-negative type, for example, expends a tremendous amount of psychic energy in intensive rationalization and self-justification for actions that foster his ambitions but do not meet the demands of his conscience.

The crusader-demagogue, committed to his cause, and ready to go down with it should public sentiment shift, would presumably not have to deal with the problem outlined above. But the opportunist-demagogue might be seen as having particular problems in resolving this dilemma. Unlike the ordinary politician who humbugs to get elected, or the Delegate who apparently will follow public opinion no matter where it goes, the opportunist-demagogue is more in the position of an activist. To some extent, he can be regarded as actually stirring up public sentiment on an issue that means little to him or on which he may be in disagreement with the public. Given normal psychological attitudes, leading the people in this manner, even more than following them, ought to take a significant psychic toll upon a politician.

Joseph McCarthy, however, if my analysis of him is correct, constitutes the extreme end of the spectrum that represents the opportunist-demagogue. Without the pressures of conscience to cope with, not bound by feelings of guilt and regret, with no need to feel that he was doing anything good or useful or important, McCarthy could do whatever the moment required. Not needing to burn up psychic energy justifying his actions to himself, McCarthy was free to turn the full force of his considerable energies outward, upon his political environment. The consequences are well known.

Problems of definition are necessarily dealt with, to some extent, in arbitrary ways. Thus, the problems involved in so complex a term as *demagogue* are not likely to be resolved in a matter of a few pages. Nonetheless, it is useful to be aware of the complexities and nuances involved while seeking to draw conclusions about the particular nature of McCarthyism. In this regard, judgments are likely to depend, at least in part, upon the ways in which McCarthy was similar to, and yet also different from, other demagogues who have moved upon the public stage and whose lives have helped shape the meaning of the term *demagogue*.

Given this preliminary analysis of demagoguery, it is now possible to ask whether one can move toward a more comprehensive view of McCarthyism. Viewing McCarthyism as a form of demagoguery, and demagoguery as a form of political leadership, what broader conclusions can be drawn about the meaning of McCarthyism?

A useful approach might involve beginning with James MacGregor Burns's definition of *leadership*—"leaders inducing followers to act for certain goals that represent the values and the motivations—the wants and needs, the aspirations and expectations—*of both leaders and the followers.*"[13] Thus, for Burns, as for most other modern students of the subject, leadership is to be found not in the traits of particular individuals, but in the interaction of people in particular circumstances.

That interaction, according to Burns, can manifest itself in two different forms: *transactional* leadership and *transformational* leadership. The former—quite common in the political arena—involves a relatively straightforward bargaining process. Leaders and followers each have certain needs they wish to satisfy, and the leader-follower relation proves able to satisfy the needs of each. The conception of the politician as playing a broker role fits in well with this particular form of leadership. "The object in these cases," Burns notes, "is not a joint effort for persons with common aims acting for the collective interests of followers but a bargain to aid the individual interests of persons or groups going their separate ways."[14] The results of such leadership are certainly not unimportant, for the daily functioning of society may depend upon the ability of leaders to succeed in such endeavors. Nonetheless, this sort of leadership is inherently limited in its ability to bring about significant change in the society. "A leadership act took place," Burns warns, "but it was not one that binds leader and follower together in a mutual and continuing pursuit of a higher purpose."[15]

In contrast, transformational leadership is a much rarer phenomenon, occurring "when one or more persons engage with others in such a way that leaders and followers raise one another to higher levels of motivation and morality."[16] Gandhi is perhaps the prime exemplar of such leadership, for his role in elevating human ideals and conduct. "The premise of this leadership," Burns maintains, "is that, whatever the separate interests persons might hold, they are presently or potentially united in the pursuit of 'higher' goals, the realization of which is tested by the achievement of significant change that represents the collective or pooled interests of leaders and followers."[17] If transactional leadership is mainly a business activity (in the sense of focusing upon bargaining and exchange), then transformational leadership is preeminently a teaching activity. It should be viewed as challenging, rather than accepting, the status quo, in its emphasis on shaping and elevating the motives, values, and goals of followers (and thereby, of the leaders also).

Drawing from Maslow's work on motivation, Piaget's and Kohlberg's work on moral development, and Rokeach's work on values, Burns concludes that "the test of leadership in all its forms . . . is the realization of purpose measured by popular needs manifested in social and human values."[18] Thus, a leader should be judged in terms of his ability to link the needs of his followers to goals that will satisfy those needs, and to move toward those goals in ways that conform to, and even elevate, the moral values of the followers. Where the needs of the people are of a relatively low order (for example, enough food to avoid starvation), the first task of leadership will, of course, be the satisfaction of such needs. But where the transactional leader might be content at this point, it would be the role of the transformational leader to point his followers toward higher needs and to help them in their satisfaction of such needs.

Ultimately, all leadership must be evaluated according to three criteria. Leaders

would have to be tested by modal values of honor and integrity—by the extent to which they advanced or thwarted fundamental standards of good conduct in humankind. They would have to be judged by the end-values of equality and justice. Finally . . . they would be judged in the balance sheet of history by their impact on the well-being of the persons whose lives they touched.[19]

In other words, leaders are to be judged in terms of their ability to satisfy the immediate needs of their followers, their ability to move followers toward higher purposes, and the means employed in these pursuits.

If one examines the approach laid down by Burns, one discovers that it corresponds well to the approach developed earlier for understanding the meaning of demagoguery. Then, too, the concern was with questions of means and ends, and ways of judging a politician's relation to these fundamental matters. Perhaps by attempting to evaluate Joseph McCarthy in terms of the criteria suggested by Burns, one could shed more light upon the nature of demagoguery.

Given the nature of transformational and transactional leadership, it seems fair to conclude that if McCarthy fell into either category, it was certainly the latter. Few, if any, would seriously pursue the argument that McCarthy was a transforming leader, raising the American people to higher motivational and moral levels. Although there was a certain amount of romanticization of McCarthy by his supporters after his death, even that view of him as a Christian defender of the West against the onslaught of godless Communism saw him primarily in a warlike, aggressive role rather than an elevating one. Anti-Communism, by its very nature, represented a negative end rather than a positive one, and therefore, was not likely to serve as a basis for raising the standards of American life.

Having examined McCarthy's own needs and the level of his moral development in earlier chapters, it seems fair to conclude that both were, on the whole, of a fairly low order. The need for glory and prestige is not likely to serve as the basis for an elevation of American society. Similarly, McCarthy's stage of moral development (at least within the political arena) was apparently fixated at the early stage of punishment orientation. A leader whose own needs and moral development is relatively low will, logically, be unable to offer potential followers more than he possesses himself.

McCarthy's career demonstrates the validity of this reasoning, for his appeals were primarily to the even lower need (on Maslow's hierarchy) of security and safety.

It is one thing to help liberate persons from a basic need, such as food or safety, so that they might be free to move up the hierarchy of needs to a level where those needs can be fulfilled, something quite different to pinion a person to an artificial need through exclusive access to that person's motive base.[20]

What Burns suggests here is that it is possible, by *manipulation,* to appeal to lower, or artificially sustained and intensified, needs. The so-called leader who engages in such practices should not be seen as a leader at all, but simply as the manipulator he is. When followers are played upon in such a way that they are blinded to alternatives and are kept from the information they need to make informed choices, there is no real leadership involved at all.

Thus, it might seem plausible initially to view McCarthy as a transactional leader brokering a deal with the American people in which he satisfied their needs for security and safety, provided his Republican party with an issue to help them ride back into power, while taking as his fee the legitimacy the party provided him and the newspaper headlines he was able to gain thereby.

However, if one doubts the existence of a domestic Communist threat to America in the 1950s, or at least the extent of such a threat, then one would be forced to conclude that McCarthy was involved in pushing the American people toward satisfaction of a need that was artificially created. Unlike the true transactional leader who presumably provides genuine goods to the people, in the form of satisfaction of genuine needs, the manipulator (or demagogue) is engaged in the manufacture of false needs and then the provision of the dubious product that will supposedly serve as a cure-all. In no sense should this be regarded as comparable to the activities of even the most ordinary politicians, engaged in the day-to-day process of keeping the government going.

Secondly, the transactional politician has as his "chief monitors" the modal values, "that is, values of means—honesty, responsibility, fairness, the honoring of commitments—without which transactional leadership would not work."[21] Needless to say, McCarthy fares exceedingly poorly when judged by this criterion. The very term *McCarthyism* implies an almost total disregard for means, a lack of concern for fairness or honest dealing. Thus, even McCarthy's supporters were driven to the formulation "I agree with Senator McCarthy's aims but I disapprove of his methods." Many of those who viewed him as doing good and important work nonetheless were not prepared to defend the means he employed in pursuit of his ends. One might well conclude, therefore, that not only did McCarthy lead his followers *downward* in motivational level, but that he did so in such a way as to undermine moral values.

Perhaps then, after the analysis of leadership completed here, one may suggest that demagoguery can be described in terms of the concepts developed by Burns. Pulling together various strands, one might conclude that demagoguery is a form of quasi leadership, involving the motivating of followers to fulfill needs lower than could be motivating them, without regard to means employed and toward no significant ends (or even towards evil ends), so as to satisfy the lower needs of the demagogue. With this definition, a basis exists for understanding a degrading kind of leadership that is perhaps not leadership at all—a kind of leadership that leaves followers less well off than they were before the leader came to power.

The final point to be made in this regard has to do with the issue of what this kind of leadership does to the so-called leader. Manipulation, Burns suggests,

> has equally serious consequences for *leaders*. Essentially they manipulate themselves in manipulating others. In concentrating on a particular "lower" need of the follower they concentrate as well on their own particular motivations that prompt them to arouse that need in a follower. . . . The more the follower's need is aroused and satisfied, the more the manipulator's motive to satisfy that need is sustained and perpetuated. Leader and led come to be locked into a symbiotic maintenance of each other's lower needs.[22]

Manipulation thus comes to degrade the leader as much as, or more than, the followers. Since the leader becomes fixated at a low level of needs and morality, his chances for attaining the level of higher needs—self-actualization—is lost. In taking advantage of the weaknesses of the people, the demagogue reinforces his own weakness, and trades important values for short-term gratification. The opportunist-demagogue, believing in nothing, seems especially susceptible to this turn of events. What was McCarthy left with after the events of December 1954?

Finally, of course, one would like to know whether a resurgence of McCarthyism in American life is possible. Burns asserts that one of the most vital aspects of leadership is that "it cannot influence people 'downward' on the need or value hierarchy without a reinforcing environment."[23] What does this say about America in the post-McCarthy era and the prospects for the rise of a demagogue similar to Joseph McCarthy?

A popular theme in American historical writing has been the recurrence of witch-hunts in our society. Beginning with the Salem witch trials of the seventeenth century, and moving on through the Illuminati scares and anti-Masonic and anti-Catholic movements of the eighteenth and nineteenth centuries, and the Palmer raids and McCarthyism in the twentieth century, America has seemed highly susceptible to mass hysteria.[24] Inevitably therefore, the question arises whether something of this nature can happen again.

From the perspective of the analysis developed in this study of Joseph McCarthy, the answer would have to be a strongly qualified yes. On the one hand, given the confluence of specific circumstances and an individual with the right motivation and resources, able to seize the opportunity, some such phenomenon could certainly occur again. On the other hand, looking at the matter in terms of probabilities, the recurrence of the particular set of circumstances that brought McCarthyism to such a peak of influence in 1950s America *and* the presence of an individual with McCarthy's unique personality seems quite improbable.

It might be argued that certain elements of the American political system do point in the direction of increasing the likelihood of a new McCarthyism. For example, it has been argued that McCarthy's rise to power represented a failure of various mediating institutions of American politics to perform their screening functions. Political parties and governmental institutions that might rightfully have been expected to prevent, or at least minimize the impact of, a phenomenon like McCarthyism did not do so. Has this situation improved in recent years?

The answer is that, quite to the contrary, political parties have declined even further in strength. McCarthy's success was due at least in part to the weak political parties that were a legacy of La Follette Progressivism. In many ways, the rest of the United States has moved in the same direction of weakened parties. Both as organizational structures and as psychological identities cuing voter behavior, parties have become much weaker over the years. In particular respect to the nominating function—traditionally at the heart of a political party's power—there has been an undercutting of party control, replaced by the influence of the mass media and interest groups. The field thus has been opened to candidates normally not acceptable to the parties' leaders, and this has traditionally been thought to increase the potential for demagogues to succeed.

Similarly, in the realm of party identification, which once operated as an extremely effective anchor in holding people in line even against the strong appeals of a demagogic figure, there has been a marked weakening in recent years. As more voters become independents and have less intense partisan feelings even when they continue to identify with a particular party, party identification loses some of its constraining power. Voters then become more susceptible to the immediate pull of such short-term forces as demagogic appeals.

Finally, the governmental institutions themselves appear to be moving toward a less controlled, more individualistic style of organization. In the House of Representatives, for example, party control has waned steadily since the early 1960s, as individual subcommittee chairmen have come to exercise more and more power on their own. In the Senate, where many long believed that an "Inner Club" exercised informal social control over the workings of that house of Congress, that club (if it ever existed) seems to have vanished. Thus, potential restraints upon demagogues (and upon mavericks in general) have been on the decline, and with that decline has come a decline in the potential sanctions that could be brought to bear upon those who violate the norms and customs of American political life.

One major countervailing force against the direction of the trends described so far involves the mass media. It may well be the case that the uncritical brand of reporting that allowed McCarthyism to come across to the American people as considerably more substantial than it appears to have been would no longer be regarded as good reporting. The mass media today may be coming to view themselves as less of a mere conduit for moving the news from news makers to news consumers. Lester Markel, a former editor for the *New York Times,* has argued that the reporter's responsibility is not simply to report the news, but to help the public reach conclusions about the truth of a matter. Faced with a Senator McCarthy holding a list of fifty-three names he claims represent Communists in the State Department, a reporter ought to have prepared a news story in which "the first sentence . . . should have stated the Senator's accusation, the second that he offered no proof of the charge."[25] A greater willingness to provide analysis and interpretation, rather than simply acting as a stenographic service for any politician looking for free publicity, may make the rise of another McCarthy somewhat less likely in the future.

Thus, institutional forces at work in American politics point in opposite directions on this question of whether the current political environment would encourage or discourage a resurgence of McCarthy-like activities. One additional psychological force ought also to be examined.

It appears to be a fact of American political life that periodically some movement from the right arises and frightens American liberals and their intellectual allies into submission. One has only to look at the current rise of the Moral Majority as a liberal bugaboo almost comparable to McCarthyism. Indeed, in the same way that liberals were willing to attribute the defeats of certain senators in 1950 to McCarthy's enormous power, the New Right was being credited with similar prowess after the Democrats' election debacle of 1980. Empirical evidence that the 1980 defeats were due to the New Right or the Moral Majority was as noticably lacking as it had been in 1950 regarding Senator McCarthy's strength. In the early months of 1981, Ronald Reagan was being viewed as an unstoppable force because he represented the views of a nation that had supposedly been captured by the New Right. Sustained opposition to the president's policies were being widely touted as a formula for defeat, and liberals were prepared to do no more than quibble about the exact size of tax cuts and budget reductions.

This tendency of liberals and intellectuals to see periodically a massive right-wing threat overwhelming the puny forces of liberalism poses some interesting questions. One thinks of a letter written by Hubert Humphrey in which he warned that one danger of McCarthyism lay in "the addiction of liberals in politics to concentrate their entire attention upon him."[26] Liberals almost seemed to allow themselves to become transfixed by

McCarthy. Certainly the defeats of some key Democratic senators in 1950 contributed to such fear, but one has to wonder why so many seasoned politicians and political observers were ready so quickly to read into such defeats proof of McCarthy's immense power. Perhaps it is not too far-fetched to suggest that there may have been an element of self-hypnosis involved, and that liberals unconsciously conspired in the rise of Mc-Carthyism.[27]

In the early 1950s, most liberals apparently resigned themselves to the nightmare of McCarthyism. Convincing themselves that McCarthyism represented a broad-based popular movement, liberals put up shamefully minimal resistance to the assaults on civil liberties led by the senator from Wisconsin. Although there was no hard evidence of extensive support for McCarthy among the public, liberals retreated into silence and occasional grumbling. Some, in fact, sought to implement the main tenets of Mc-Carthyism while avoiding only its more blatantly disagreeable aspects.

Why were liberals so easily frightened by such a chimera? Perhaps liberals periodically tire of their self-proclaimed role as innovators of social change.[28] They may therefore have need, from time to time, of an opportunity to retire from political combat and thereby renew their energies.

But the suffering of those whom the liberals see themselves as aiding does not stop simply because liberals need a respite. The liberals' awareness of that continued suffering makes quiescence psychologically uncomfortable for them. What better rationalization for surrender then, than to conjure up in one's mind some phantasm of right-wing power so overwhelming that it is pointless even to attempt to challenge it? While the "need for control" has been pointed to as an important aspect of political socialization, it may well be the case that there is also at work, at least at some times, a comparable need for loss of control.[29]

The surrender involved in this loss of control may well be a necessary prerequisite to the return of the liberals with new ideas for reform and change. Thus, a self-induced feeling of impotence may be a periodic requirement for liberals if they are to continue to function as a force for change in society.

This suggests that liberals will indeed continue to give way before conservative or right-wing power on a regular basis, and this *might* amount to a new yielding to McCarthyism at some point. Still, without the particular set of political circumstances that gave McCarthy his legitimacy, and without a political leader who closely reproduces McCarthy's political style, a recurrence of the phenomenon known as McCarthyism does not seem likely to occur again. A German philosopher once remarked that history tends to repeat itself—the first time as tragedy, the second time as farce. Perhaps America can hope that it was fortunate enough, in the case of Joe McCarthy and McCarthyism, to have undergone both at once.

## Notes

1. Fred I. Greenstein and Nelson W. Polsby, eds., *Handbook of Political Science,* vol. 5 (Reading, Mass.: Addison-Wesley, 1975), p. 41.

2. Gene L. Mason and Dean Jaros, "Alienation and Support for Demagogues," *Polity* 1 (Summer 1969): 485.

3. *Oxford English Dictionary,* 1st ed. (1933; rpt., 1961), s.v. "demagogue."

4. Jack C. Plano and Milton Greenberg, *The American Political Dictionary,* 4th ed. (New York: Holt, Rinehart and Winston, 1976), p. 118.

5. William Safire, *The New Language of Politics,* rev. ed. (New York: Collier Books, 1972), p. 151.

6. David H. Bennett, *Demagogues in the Depression* (New Brunswick, N.J.: Rutgers University Press, 1969), p. 4.

7. Mason and Jaros, "Alienation and Support," p. 499.

8. Buckley, and Bozell, *McCarthy and Enemies,* p. 302.

9. H. L. Mencken, "Why Nobody Loves a Politician," *Liberty,* 27 October 1934, reprinted in *New York Times,* 13 September 1980.

10. Bennett, *Demagogues in the Depression,* p. 7.

11. Frank R. Kent, *The Great Game of Politics* (Garden City, N.Y.: Doubleday and Company, 1923), pp. 196–97.

12. Wahlke et al., *Legislative System,* chap. 12.

13. Burns, *Leadership,* p. 19.

14. Ibid., p. 425.

15. Ibid., p. 20.

16. Ibid.

17. Ibid., pp. 425–26.

18. Ibid., p. 251.

19. Ibid., p. 426.

20. Ibid., p. 458.

21. Ibid., p. 426.

22. Ibid., p. 458.

23. Ibid., p. 44.

24. Richard Hofstadter, *The Paranoid Style in American Politics* (New York: Vintage Books, 1964), chap. 1.

25. Lester Markel, *What You Don't Know Can Hurt You* (New York: Quadrangle Press, 1972), pp. 164–65.

26. Fried, *Men Against McCarthy,* p. 313.

27. Will Herberg, as far back as 1954, was already suggesting that liberals had "acted as if driven by some inner compulsion to build up McCarthy and McCarthyism as a force in the land," and had seemed "hypnotized by the evil genius from Wisconsin" (see "Hitler and McCarthy," p. 15).

28. The historiography of the Progressive Movement, for example, has as one of its most important questions "What Happened to the Progressive Movement in the 1920s?" (Arthur S. Link, *American Historical Review,* 64, July 1959, 833–851). Richard Hofstadter, *The Age of Reform* (New York: Vintage Books, 1955), refers to the "Entr'Acte" of the 1920s (p. 282). William E. Leuchtenberg, *The Perils of Prosperity, 1914–1932* (Chicago: University of Chicago Press, 1958) describes "Tired Radicals" (chap. 7). Otis L. Graham, Jr., *An Encore for Reform: The Old Progressives and the New Deal* (New York: Oxford University Press, 1967), points to a "Farewell to Reform" (chap. 5). Each tries to explain the evident loss of energy and commitment among liberals after nearly two decades of reformist fervor.

29. Renshon, *Psychological Needs and Political Behavior,* analyzes the need for control.

# Works Cited

## Joseph McCarthy

Alexander, Jack. "The Senate's Most Remarkable Upstart." *Saturday Evening Post,* 9 August 1947, pp. 15–17, 52–58.

Anderson, Clinton P., with Milton Viorst. *Outsider in the Senate: Senator Clinton Anderson's Memoirs.* New York: World Publishing, 1970.

Anderson, Jack, and Ronald May. *McCarthy: The Man, the Senator, the "Ism."* Boston: Beacon Press, 1952.

Bayley, Edwin R. *Joe McCarthy and the Press.* Madison: University of Wisconsin Press, 1981.

Bell, Daniel, ed. *The New American Right.* New York: Criterion, 1955.

———, ed. *The Radical Right.* Garden City, N.Y.: Doubleday, 1963.

Buckley, William F., Jr., and L. Brent Bozell. *McCarthy and His Enemies.* Chicago: Henry Regnery, 1954.

Cohn, Roy. *McCarthy.* New York: New American Library, 1968.

Cook, Fred J. *The Nightmare Decade: The Life and Times of Senator Joe McCarthy.* New York: Random House, 1971.

Crosby, Donald F. *God, Church, and Flag: Senator Joseph R. McCarthy and the Catholic Church, 1950–1957.* Chapel Hill: University of North Carolina Press, 1978.

Douglas, Paul H. *In the Fullness of Time.* New York: Harcourt Brace Jovanovich, 1972.

Ewald, William Bragg, Jr. *Who Killed Joe McCarthy?* New York: Simon and Schuster, 1984.

Feuerlicht, Roberta S. *Joe McCarthy and McCarthyism: The Hate That Haunts America.* New York: McGraw-Hill, 1972.

Freeland, Richard M. *The Truman Doctrine and the Origins of McCarthyism.* New York: Alfred Knopf, 1971.

Fried, Richard M. *Men Against McCarthy.* New York: Columbia University Press, 1976.

Goldman, Eric F. *The Crucial Decade—and After: America, 1945–1960.* New York: Vintage Books, 1960.

———. "The Rise of a Demagogue." *New York Times Book Review,* 11 April 1982, pp. 9, 19.

Goldston, Robert C. *The American Nightmare*. Indianapolis: Bobbs-Merrill, 1973.

Greenstein, Fred I. *The Hidden-Hand Presidency: Eisenhower as Leader*. New York: Basic Books, 1982.

Griffith, Robert. "The Notorious Baiter." *Progressive* (November 1982): 56–57.

———. *The Politics of Fear: Joseph R. McCarthy and the Senate*. Lexington: University of Kentucky Press, 1970.

Harper, Alan D. *The Politics of Loyalty: The White House and the Communist Issue, 1946–1952*. Westport, Conn.: Greenwood Press, 1969.

Herberg, Will. "McCarthy and Hitler: A Delusive Parallel." *New Republic*, 23 August 1954, pp. 13–15.

Latham, Earl. *The Communist Controversy in Washington: From the New Deal to McCarthy*. Cambridge: Harvard University Press, 1966.

Lubell, Samuel. *The Future of American Politics*. 2d ed. Garden City, N.Y.: Doubleday, 1956.

Luthin, Reinhard. *American Demagogues*. Boston: Beacon Press, 1954.

McPherson, Harry. *A Political Education*. Boston: Little, Brown, 1972.

Mooney, Booth. *The Politicians*. Philadelphia: Lippincott, 1970.

Nevins, Allan. *Herbert H. Lehman and His Era*. New York: Charles Scribner's Sons, 1963.

O'Brien, Michael. "McCarthy and McCarthyism: The Cedric Parker Case, November 1949." In *The Specter: Original Essays on the Cold War and the Origins of McCarthyism,* edited by Robert Griffith and Athan Theoharis. New York: New Viewpoints, 1974.

———. *McCarthy and McCarthyism in Wisconsin*. Columbia: University of Missouri Press, 1980.

Oshinsky, David M. *A Conspiracy So Immense: The World of Joe McCarthy*. New York: Free Press, 1983.

———. *Senator Joseph McCarthy and the American Labor Movement*. Columbia: University of Missouri Press, 1976.

Patterson, James T. *Mr. Republican: A Biography of Robert A. Taft*. Boston: Houghton Mifflin, 1972.

Polsby, Nelson W. "Towards an Explanation of McCarthyism." *Political Studies* 8 (October 1960): 250–71.

Potter, Charles. *Days of Shame*. New York: Coward-McCann, 1965.

Reeves, Thomas C. *The Life and Times of Joe McCarthy*. New York: Stein and Day, 1982.

Rogin, Michael Paul. *The Intellectuals and McCarthy: The Radical Specter*. Cambridge: MIT Press, 1967.

Rorty, James, and Moshe Decter. *McCarthy and the Communists*. Boston: Beacon Press, 1954.

Rovere, Richard. "McCarthy: As National Demagogue." In *The Meaning of McCarthyism,* 2d ed., edited by Earl Latham. Lexington, Mass: D. C. Heath, 1973.

———. *Senator Joe McCarthy*. New York: Harcourt, Brace, 1959.

Shaffer, Samuel. *On and Off the Floor.* New York: Newsweek Books, 1980.

Smith, Geoffrey, S. " 'Harry, We Hardly Knew You': Revisionism, Politics and Diplomacy, 1945–1954." *American Political Science Review* 70 (March 1976): 560–82.

Smith, Margaret Chase, with William C. Lewis, Jr. *Declaration of Conscience.* Garden City, N.Y.: Doubleday, 1972.

Straight, Michael. *Trial by Television.* Boston: Beacon Press, 1954.

Theoharis, Athan. "The Politics of Scholarship: Liberals, Anti-Communism, and McCarthyism." In *The Specter: Original Essays on the Cold War and the Origins of McCarthyism,* edited by Robert Griffith and Athan Theoharis. New York: New Viewpoints, 1974.

———. *Seeds of Repression: Harry S. Truman and the Origins of McCarthyism.* Chicago: Quadrangle, 1971.

Thomas, Lately. *When Even Angels Wept.* New York: William Morrow, 1973.

Watkins, Arthur V. *Enough Rope.* Englewood Cliffs, N.J.: Prentice-Hall, 1969.

Wechsler, James A. *Reflections of an Angry Middle-Aged Editor.* New York: Random House, 1960.

White, William S. *The Taft Story.* New York: Harper and Brothers, 1954.

Wilkes, Paul. "Leonard Boudin: The Left's Lawyer's Lawyer." *New York Times Magazine,* 14 November 1971.

Williams, Edward Bennett. *One Man's Freedom.* New York: Atheneum, 1962.

## Personality and Politics

Axelrod, Robert, ed. *Structure of Decision: The Cognitive Maps of Political Elites.* Princeton: Princeton University Press, 1976.

Barber, James David. "Adult Identity and Presidential Style: The Rhetorical Emphasis." *Daedalus* 97 (Summer 1968): 938–68.

———. "Classifying and Predicting Presidential Styles: Two 'Weak' Presidents." *Journal of Social Issues* 24 (July 1968): 51–80.

———. *The Lawmakers: Recruitment and Adaptation to Legislative Life.* New Haven: Yale University Press, 1965.

———. "The President and His Friends." *American Political Science Association Annual Meeting.* New York, 1969.

———. *The Presidential Character: Predicting Performance in the White House.* Englewood Cliffs, N.J.: Prentice-Hall, 1972.

———. "Strategies for Understanding Politicians." *American Journal of Political Science* 18 (May 1974): 443–67.

Bay, Christian. *The Structure of Human Freedom.* Stanford: Stanford University Press, 1958.

Bennett, W. Lance. *The Political Mind and the Political Environment.* Lexington, Mass.: Lexington Books, 1975.

———. *Public Opinion in American Politics.* New York: Harcourt Brace Jovanovich, 1980.

Berkowitz, Leonard. *Aggression: A Social Psychological Analysis.* New York: McGraw-Hill, 1962.

Browning, Rufus P. "The Interaction of Personality and Political System in Decisions to Run for Office: Some Data and a Simulation Technique." *Journal of Social Issues* 24 (July 1968): 93–109.

Burns, James MacGregor. *Leadership.* New York: Harper and Row, 1978.

Christie, Richard, and Florence L. Geis. *Studies in Machiavellianism.* New York: Academic Press, 1970.

Connell, R. W. *The Child's Construction of Politics.* Melbourne: Melbourne University Press, 1971.

Converse, Philip. "The Nature of Belief Systems in Mass Publics." In *Ideology and Discontent,* edited by David E. Apter. New York: Free Press, 1964.

Crosby, Faye, and Travis L. Crosby. "Psychobiography and Psychohistory." In *The Handbook of Political Behavior,* vol. 1, edited by Samuel L. Long. New York: Plenum Press, 1981.

Davies, James C. *Human Nature in Politics.* New York: John Wiley, 1963.

Dawson, Richard E., Kenneth Prewitt, and Karen S. Dawson, *Political Socialization.* 2d ed. Boston: Little, Brown, 1977.

Easton, David. *Children in the Political System.* New York: McGraw-Hill, 1969.

Edinger, Lewis. "Political Science and Political Biography." In *Political Leadership: Readings for an Emerging Field,* edited by Glenn Paige. New York: Free Press, 1972.

Etheredge, Lloyd. "Hardball Politics: A Model." *Political Psychology* 1 (Spring 1979): 3–26.

Flavell, J. H. *The Developmental Psychology of Jean Piaget.* Princeton: Van Nostrand, 1963.

Geis, Florence. "Machiavellianism." In *Dimensions of Personality,* edited by Harvey London and John E. Exner, Jr. New York: Wiley, 1978.

George, Alexander. "Assessing Presidential Character." *World Politics* 26 (January 1974): 234–82.

———. "Some Uses of Dynamic Psychology in Political Biography: Case Materials on Woodrow Wilson." In *A Source Book for the Study of Personality and Politics,* edited by Fred I. Greenstein and Michael Lerner. Chicago: Markham, 1971.

———, and Juliette L. George. *Woodrow Wilson and Colonel House.* New York: John Day, 1956.

Glad, Betty. "The Role of Psychoanalytical Biography in Political Science." *American Political Science Association Annual Meeting.* Washington, D.C., 1968.

Greenstein, Fred I. "Personality and Politics." In *Handbook of Political Science,* vol. 2, edited by Fred I. Greenstein and Nelson W. Polsby. Reading, Mass.: Addison-Wesley, 1975.

———. *Personality and Politics.* New York: W. W. Norton, 1975.

———. "Political Psychology: A Pluralistic Universe." In *Handbook of Political Psychology,* edited by Jeanne N. Knutson. San Francisco: Josey-Bass, 1973.

Hargrove, Erwin. "Presidential Personality and Revisionist Views of the Presidency." *American Journal of Political Science* 17 (November 1973): 819–35.

Hyman, Herbert H. *Political Socialization*. New York: Free Press, 1959.

Inglehart, Ronald. "The Silent Revolution in Europe: Intergenerational Change in Post-Industrial Societies." *American Political Science Review* 65 (December 1971): 991–1017.

Kagan, Jerome. "Developmental Studies in Reflection and Analysis." In *Perceptual Development in Children,* edited by Aline H. Kidd and Jeanne L. Riviere. New York: International Universities Press, 1966.

———. "Impulsive and Reflective Children." In *Learning and the Educational Process,* edited by J. Krumboltz. Chicago: Rand-McNally, 1965.

———, H. A. Moss, and I. E. Siegel. "Psychological Significance of Styles of Conceptualization." In *Basic Cognitive Processes,* edited by J. C. Wright and Jerome Kagan. Monographs of the Society for Research in Child Development, 28, no. 2, 1963.

———, Leslie Pearson, and Lois Welch. "Conceptual Impulsivity and Inductive Reasoning." *Child Development* 37 (September 1966): 583–94.

———, Bernice L. Rosman, Deborah Day, Joseph Albert, and William Phillips. "Information Processing in the Child: Significance of Analytic and Reflective Attitudes." *Psychological Monographs: General and Applied* 78 (1964).

Katz, Daniel. "Patterns of Leadership." In *Handbook of Political Psychology,* edited by Jeanne N. Knutson. San Francisco: Josey-Bass, 1973.

Kipnis, David. *Character Structure and Impulsiveness*. New York: Academic Press, 1971.

Knutson, Jeanne N. *The Human Basis of the Polity*. Chicago: Aldine-Atherton, 1972.

———. "Personality in the Study of Politics." In *Handbook of Political Psychology,* edited by Jeanne N. Knutson. San Francisco: Josey-Bass, 1973.

———. "Prepolitical Ideologies: The Basis of Political Learning." In *The Politics of Future Citizens,* edited by Richard G. Niemi. San Francisco: Josey-Bass, 1974.

Kohlberg, Lawrence. "Moral Development." In *International Encyclopedia of the Social Sciences,* vol. 10. New York Macmillan and Free Press, 1968.

———. "Stage and Sequence: The Cognitive-Developmental Approach to Socialization." In *Handbook of Socialization Theory and Research,* edited by David A. Goslin. Chicago: Rand-McNally, 1969.

Lane, Robert. *Political Ideology*. New York: Free Press, 1962.

———. *Political Man*. New York: Free Press, 1972.

———. *Political Thinking and Consciousness*. Chicago: Markham, 1969.

Langton, Kenneth. *Political Socialization*. New York: Oxford University Press, 1969.

Lasswell, Harold. *Power and Personality*. New York: W. W. Norton, 1948.

———. *Psychopathology and Politics*. 1930. Reprint. New York: Viking Press, 1960.

Lawrence, Paul R., and John A. Seiler, eds. *Organizational Behavior and Administration*. Rev. ed. Homewood, Ill.: Dorsey Press, 1965.

Leites, Nathan. *The Operational Code of the Politburo*. New York: McGraw-Hill, 1951.

Marsh, Alan. "The 'Silent Revolution,' Value Priorities, and the Quality of Life in Britain." *American Political Science Review* 69 (March 1975): 21–30.

Maslow, Abraham H. *Motivation and Personality*. 2d ed. New York: Harper and Row, 1954.

———. "A Theory of Human Motivation." In *Dominance, Self-Esteem, Self-Actualization: The Germinal Papers of A. H. Maslow*, edited by Richard J. Lowry. Monterey, Calif.: Brooks/Cole, 1973.

Merelman, Richard M. "The Development of Policy Thinking in Adolescence." *American Political Science Review* 65 (December 1971): 1033–47.

———. "The Development of Political Ideology: A Framework for the Analysis of Political Socialization." *American Political Science Review* 63 (September 1969): 750–67.

Nelson, Michael. "The Psychological Presidency." In *The Presidency and the Political System*, edited by Michael Nelson. Washington, D.C.: CQ Press, 1984.

Payne, James L., and Oliver H. Woshinsky. "Incentives for Political Participation." *World Politics* 24 (July 1972): 518–46.

———, Oliver H. Woshinsky, Eric P. Veblen, William H. Coogan, and Gene E. Bigler. *The Motivation of Politicians*. Chicago: Nelson-Hall, 1984.

Piaget, Jean. *The Child's Conception of the World*. London: Routledge and Kegan Paul, 1951.

———. *The Construction of Reality in the Child*. New York: Basic Books, 1954.

———. *The Moral Judgment of the Child*. Glencoe, Ill.: Free Press, 1948.

Putnam, Robert. *The Beliefs of Politicians*. New Haven: Yale University Press, 1973.

Qualls, James H. "Barber's Typological Analysis of Political Leaders." *American Political Science Review* 71 (March 1977): 182–211.

Renshon, Stanley Allen. *Psychological Needs and Political Behavior*. New York: Free Press, 1974.

Rogow, Arnold, and Harold Lasswell. *Power, Corruption and Rectitude*. Englewood Cliffs, N.J.: Prentice-Hall, 1963.

Rokeach, Milton. *The Open and Closed Mind*. New York: Basic Books, 1960.

Sartori, Giovanni. "Politics, Ideology, and Belief Systems." *American Political Science Review* 63 (June 1969): 398–411.

Sears, Robert R. "Identification as a Form of Behavioral Development." In *The Concept of Development*, edited by Dale B. Harris. Minneapolis: University of Minnesota Press, 1957.

Shapiro, David. *Neurotic Styles*. New York: Basic Books, 1965.

Tucker, Robert C. "The Georges' Wilson Reconsidered: An Essay on Psychobiography." *American Political Science Review* 71 (June 1977): 606–18.

Whiting, John, and Irwin L. Child. *Child Training and Personality*. New Haven: Yale University Press, 1953.

Winter, David G. *The Power Motive*. New York: Free Press, 1973.


## General

Banfield, Edward C., and James Q. Wilson. *City Politics*. New York: Vintage Books, 1963.

Bennett, David H. *Demagogues in the Depression*. New Brunswick, N.J.: Rutgers University Press, 1969.

Berelson, Bernard R., Paul F. Lazarsfeld, and William N. McPhee. *Voting: A Study in Opinion Formation in a Presidential Campaign*. Chicago: University of Chicago Press, 1954.

Graham, Otis L., Jr. *An Encore for Reform: The Old Progressives and the New Deal*. New York: Oxford University Press, 1967.

Hofstadter, Richard. *The Age of Reform*. New York: Vintage Books, 1955.

———. *The Idea of a Party System: The Rise of Legitimate Opposition in the United States, 1740–1840*. Berkeley and Los Angeles: University of California Press, 1970.

———. *The Paranoid Style in American Politics*. New York: Vintage Books, 1964.

Huitt, Ralph K. "The Outsider in the Senate: An Alternative Role." *American Political Science Review* 55 (September 1961): 566–75.

Kent, Frank R. *The Great Game of Politics*. Garden City, N.Y.: Doubleday and Company, 1923.

Key, V. O., Jr. *Politics, Parties and Pressure Groups*. 5th ed. New York: Thomas Y. Crowell, 1964.

Leuchtenberg, William W. *The Perils of Prosperity, 1914–1932*. Chicago: University of Chicago Press, 1958.

Link, Arthur S. "What Happened to the Progressive Movement in the 1920s?" *American Historical Review* 64 (July 1959): 833–51.

Lipset, Seymour Martin, Martin Trow, and James S. Coleman. *Union Democracy*. Glencoe, Ill.: Free Press, 1956.

Markel, Lester. *What You Don't Know Can Hurt You*. New York: Quadrangle Press, 1972.

Mason, Gene L., and Dean Jaros. "Alienation and Support for Demagogues." *Polity* 1 (Summer 1969): 479–500.

Matthews, Donald R. "Can the Outsider's Role Be Legitimate?" *American Political Science Review* 55 (December 1961): 882–83.

———. *U.S. Senators and Their World*. Chapel Hill: University of North Carolina Press, 1960.

Mencken, H. L. "Why Nobody Loves a Politician." *Liberty,* 27 October 1934. Reprinted in the *New York Times,* 13 September 1980, p. 21.

Plano, Jack C., and Milton Greenberg. *The American Political Dictionary*. 4th ed. New York: Holt, Rinehart and Winston, 1976.

Rieselbach, Leroy N. *Congressional Politics*. New York: McGraw-Hill, 1973.

Safire, William. *The New Language of Politics*. Rev. ed. New York: Collier Books, 1972.

Smith, Robert P. *Tiger in the Senate*. Garden City, N.Y.: Doubleday, 1962.

Wahlke, John C., Heinz Eulau, William Buchanan, and LeRoy C. Ferguson. *The Legislative System*. New York: Wiley, 1962.

# Index

167